Wicked
FLAGSTAFF

SUSAN JOHNSON

THE
History
PRESS

Published by The History Press
Charleston, SC
www.historypress.com

Front cover, background, top: Sanborn Fire Insurance Map. *Sanborn Map Company*; *bottom*: The wooden structures of Old Town Flagstaff, looking north toward the Peaks, 1888. *Library of Congress.*
Clockwise from top left: Governor Wolfley, who was as unpopular with all of Arizona as he was in Flagstaff. *Library of Congress*; Log train in woods near Flagstaff. *Library of Congress*; Commodore Perry Owens before he was elected sheriff of Navajo County. *Wikipedia*; A man and woman on horseback, Fort Verde. *Library of Congress.*
Back cover, background: Snow on the San Francisco Peaks. *Author's collection.*
Clockwise from bottom left: Pluto Dome at Lowell Observatory. *Library of Congress*; Two women in uniform and on horseback, Fort Verde, Arizona. *Library of Congress.*

First published 2024

Manufactured in the United States

ISBN 9781467156394

Library of Congress Control Number: 2024937601

Notice: The information in this book is true and complete to the best of our knowledge. It is offered without guarantee on the part of the author or The History Press. The author and The History Press disclaim all liability in connection with the use of this book.

In loving tribute to the quirky little mountain town my family's called home for the past thirty-five years. While not as wicked as it once was, Flagstaff is still wonderfully weird and freaky.

And for my son, Nick—who does his part to keep it that way. Boo!

CONTENTS

ACKNOWLEDGEMENTS

*E*very book I've read on Flagstaff's early history cites the Babbitts, the Riordans and Platt Cline somewhere in the text. The former were among the early settlers who hammered out an infrastructure for this boomtown seeded by the railroad and the lumber mills. Fortunately, members of both families left written records that their descendants have shared. Cline was the longtime editor of the *Daily Sun*, and he often credited the paper and his reporters for the detailed history of how this tiny town grew into a thriving, diversified city in northern Arizona. I've relied on both of his books to get an overview of several chapters within. I'm grateful to Mr. Cline—as well as the pioneer families and early settlers— for appreciating history enough to preserve it.

Besides the people from years gone by, there are those in the present who always respond to pleas for help. Many thanks to our public library staff, especially Mary and Zanna, for their assistance in scanning old newspaper articles. And another thank-you to the staff of the Special Collections Department at Northern Arizona University who tend to the images and history of our eclectic town. Finally, a big debt of gratitude to Chris Etling, editor of the *Arizona Daily Sun*, for his continued generosity in allowing the use of images from past issues of the newspaper. I've grown to appreciate how important our local news is in educating us all.

While most chapters are rooted in Flagstaff, several are more loosely connected. Commodore Perry Owens was sheriff of Apache County, which is east of here. He spent his later years in Seligman, which is to the west. However, Owens is buried in Citizens Cemetery, so the town has some claim on the man and his fascinating life. Ditto the victims of TWA Flight 2, whose remains are interred in a mass grave at Citizens. The tragedy occurred miles north in the skies above the Grand Canyon, but Flagstaff was affected in a myriad of ways. Many stories were inspired by walks through Citizens and Calvary Cemeteries. The Northern Arizona Pioneer Historical Society occasionally hosts fundraisers that allow the public to meander through one or the other. I've participated in several events and have gathered information provided by the descendants of those buried within.

This book is titled *Wicked Flagstaff*, and while some chapters' ties to immorality, devilishness and/or wrongdoing are obvious, a few may have the reader scratching her head. I hope by the time she's done reading the theme becomes clear. I'm grateful for the suggestions from family, friends and our wonderfully frightful guides at Freaky Foot Tours for their ideas of historical depravity that are now included in this book.

As I combed through sources, I took a look at saved notes from years ago. When writing both *Flagstaff's Walkup Family Tragedy* and *Haunted Flagstaff*, I was fortunate to connect with other locals who shared my passion for the town's quirky history. Some handwritten notes weren't completely sourced (I've gotten better at this in the intervening years!), so a few endnotes might be lacking. But thank you to everyone who's been willing to tell tales and share secrets with a relative stranger. I'm also grateful to members of the Northern Arizona Pioneer Historical Society for their conversations, emails and advice on good sources to research. I've gathered inspiration from the group's past fundraisers, especially the aforementioned cemetery tours, and brown-bag lectures held at Riordan.

Thank you once again to Laurie Krill, my editor at The History Press. You are the best! Everyone at THP works together to turn out these incredible books, and I appreciate you all so much.

I mentioned friends and family earlier. Besides volunteering as a critical ear, mine are a wonderful web of support and comic relief. Flagstaff's Write Time Writers continues to meet via Zoom, since several members have relocated, and the writing from our group never fails to amaze me. My son, Nick, accompanied me on a jaunt westward to search for info on Commodore Perry Owens, and we had a great time. And many thanks to Martha Shideler, who was there for the Abney trial and also had a close brush with the 1956 Grand Canyon tragedy. Martha shared her memories with me, making both events come alive, and along the way found an incredible new source on the Canyon disaster. And to those who asked about the book and bolstered my flagging energy at just the right time, thank you thank you! Marsha, Steve, Tim, Dave, Rosie, John and Judy—you all are the best of friends and family, and I appreciate each and every one of you!

And finally, thank you again to my sweet son, Nick. I wish your dad were here for the ride, but I'm sure he's watching both our antics with a smile.

INTRODUCTION

I have written two other books on my adopted hometown for The History Press. At the beginnings of both, I clarify that the tales within—like these in *Wicked Flagstaff*—date from the mid-1800s up to more recent times. These are Anglicized stories, history from the point of view of the white settlers who arrived as the railroad came through. I could not and would not attempt to detail the rich heritage of the various Native American tribes that have lived here for centuries. There are places in the book where our paths intersect, but these accounts are heavily influenced by the Anglo recording of events. There are plenty of excellent books available on Native American history, and I urge anyone so inclined to seek them out and read them.

The taming of the Wild West is the stuff Americans grew up on, especially those of us over the age of sixty. The television shows I sat glued to as a child were of the ilk of Roy Rogers, *Bonanza* and Daniel Boone. These romantic depictions of cowboys and Indians, shootouts and saloons were limited and sanitized versions of what it really was like—but we didn't know that! The deeper I've delved into Arizona's history and that of the early pioneers, the blurrier the lines have become between the hero and the villain. However, the past is infinitely more interesting and alive when we don't bury the "wickedness" that lives within these colorful characters and situations.

A brief history of northern Arizona is necessary to set the stage for the stories within *Wicked Flagstaff*. With the end of the Mexican-American War in 1848, Mexico ceded vast acres of land to the United States. The

Treaty of Guadalupe Hidalgo deeded the spoils, which included parts of today's Texas, New Mexico, Utah, Nevada, California and Arizona, to the Union. Exploration of these newly acquired territories became the order of the next ten years, and several key expeditions traversed the northlands during the 1850s. Led by experienced men such as Captain Lorenzo Sitgreaves, Lieutenants Amiel Whipple and Edward Beale and mountain guide Antoine Leroux, these treks provided a wealth of information to the U.S. government. Washington, D.C., wanted details on what the terrain was like in the West, what resources could be found here and how to deal with the Native Americans who called this land their home. To that end, these expeditions were composed of mappers, biologists, geologists and anthropologists, who, along with the exploration leaders, carefully recorded their findings. However, the main purpose was scouting a northern route that would extend some 1,200 miles from the Midwest to the Pacific Ocean.[1]

Railways already existed in the eastern states and were used for intercity travel and trade. While there was debate over laying a track all the way to California, the feasibility of such was kept in mind by the early explorers. Lieutenant Sitgreaves led the first expedition across the thirty-fifth parallel in 1853, but it was Lieutenant Whipple who was charged with laying out a rail route. Basically following Sitgreaves's trail, he found the land amenable to undertaking the challenging task. He miscalculated the cost of laying the track by some $75 million though, causing the enterprise to be placed on hold. It was almost thirty years later—after many stops and starts and complicated agreements—that the first train chugged into Flagstaff on its way to the West Coast. That day was August 1, 1882, and—while it would take a few years—it marked the beginnings of taming the wild West. Not only were goods and merchandise more easily exchanged, but newspapers and mail also began to arrive somewhat reliably, as did travelers from the East.

The second auspicious event occurred nineteen days later when E.E. Ayers opened the doors to his sawmill, a business that sustained the town for decades. Flagstaff sits in the middle of the largest contingent Ponderosa pine forest west of the Mississippi (some say all of the United States). In a time when whole towns were made of wood and railroad ties were a necessity, Flagstaff was sitting in a gold mine. It's hard to overstress how important the mill was to the growth and success of the settlement. Men who earned a steady paycheck could afford to start a family. Families required schools, mercantile stores, doctors, grocers and churches. While many promising railroad encampments turned into ghost towns, Flagstaff dug in its heels

Snow on the San Francisco Peaks. Flagstaff still surprises those who think Arizona is only a desert full of cacti and scrub. *Author's collection.*

and steered its way toward stability and prosperity. Some chapters of *Wicked Flagstaff* are about the challenges local officials faced as they corralled the citizenry and enacted laws with these goals in mind. The West wasn't called wild for nothing!

Besides the aforementioned events, one has to acknowledge the part geography played in the town's success and survival. Northern Arizona's temperate climate, four distinct seasons and clean mountain air made it an attractive place to live and visit year-round. Famed western author Zane Grey was promoting Flagstaff to tourists—and the tourist industry to the town—as early as 1910. When Grey's popular novel *The Call of the Canyon* was made into a movie, visitors flocked to this area. They wanted to experience the wide-open spaces and rugged wilderness that captivated the author. Sometime around 1920, Hollywood came calling. The big production companies didn't relocate here, but they used the town to stage the popular westerns that were filmed on the reservation. With the Grand Canyon to the north, Oak Creek Canyon and Sedona to the south and Native American ruins and colorful mesas all around, the town had something for everyone.[2]

This same geography also kept the area semi-isolated from the rest of the state. Flagstaff sits at 6,909 feet elevation, at the base of the San Francisco Peaks. It is a mountain town at the base of the mountains, which made it somewhat inaccessible—or at least difficult enough to keep out the faint of heart. Whether this gulf contributed to Flagstaff becoming a very different town from those in southern Arizona is debatable. I'm one who believes geography was a significant factor, especially in the 1880s and 1890s, when identities were being formed. Separated from the wilder, more desperate elements in Phoenix and Tucson, Flag succeeded in cultivating an air of education and leisure. When automobile travel came into vogue and highways were commonplace, the town already had a grasp on its image and priorities. The locals seriously lobbied Percival Lowell to establish his observatory here atop Mars Hill. Later, in the 1920s, Harold Colton and his wife, Mary Russell, settled on Flagstaff as the location for the Museum of Northern Arizona. Both of these institutions are world-class and renowned in their respective fields. Northern Arizona University (NAU) grew out of the Teachers College, and there's more on that story in chapter 4. Flagstaff built an eclectic nine-hole golf course–country club just north of town in the 1920s that drew summer visitors from several states. These are just a few examples of the people and places the town courted to become part of its distinctive fabric.

The early pioneers who became the town fathers also left their mark. Technically, ranchers and sheepherders such as Thomas McMillian, Frank Hart and John Elden were the first white settlers, staking their claims around the 1870s. In the mid-1880s, as the settlement was growing, the Babbitts, the Riordans, the Brannens and others built the businesses and infrastructure that morphed Flagstaff into a town. These same men (they were mostly men save for a few rogue women!) also sat on the town councils that enacted the first charters and regulations. They were family men—businessmen—who contributed to the town's well-being above and beyond providing stable jobs. They built churches, schools and roads and invested in finding water sources and laying an electrical grid. While one or two were occasionally portrayed as heavy-handed, it was rare to read any negative press about them in the early years.

The collection of stories in *Wicked Flagstaff* draws from characters and events that have remained unexplored in one aspect or another. Some stem from truly wicked deeds, like the murders of Dutch May Prescott in 1915 and Sarah Saganitso in 1987. Other stories, such as refining the "blue laws" and moving the town cemetery, are quirky tales with plenty of playful wickedness intertwined in the action. The chapters follow a rough timeline from early days to more recent, although there's some overlap. Finally, the reader will notice that I occasionally use "Flag" instead of Flagstaff. It's a local habit, universally accepted although sometimes disparaged, that I personally like.

So find your favorite reading chair, pour yourself a drink and sit back and enjoy the irreverent tales in *Wicked Flagstaff.* I hope you find them enlightening and entertaining. More than that, I hope you come to appreciate the quirky—and often bull-headed—characters who built our small town into the city it is today.

1
TAMING THE TOWN

The first train chugged its way through Flagstaff on August 1, 1882. Two and a half weeks later, another whistle was heard: the E.E. Ayers sawmill had officially opened for business. These two events gave the tiny railroad settlement known as Antelope Park a solid foundation and real advantage over other transient towns along the rail lines. The mill employed about 250 men and was turning out lumber at incredible speed. The trains that stopped at the boxcar that doubled as the town's station were fairly dependable. They carried in the mail along with merchandise and travelers and took away the same to another location down the line. With this giant step into the civilized world, the town looked for ways to leave the wildness of the West behind. But it would not be an easy task.

Like other boomtowns, Antelope Park seemingly sprang up overnight as the front men for the railways slowly made their way toward the Pacific coast. Some businesses sprouting up under the canvas tents sold much-needed merchandise, such as clothing and footwear. Many more were makeshift saloons, gambling arenas, tents of ill-repute and the like. This is not to paint the men's need for recreation as trivial. However, these boomtowns were widely regarded as seedy and had reputations as being hardscrabble and violent. An article in *Harper's Magazine* summed it up this way: "Every temporary terminus of track laying became a city; wicked, wonderful and short-lived." The writer went on to declare, "The Pacific railways have been responsible for more and worse towns than any other single cause."[3]

This photo from 1888 shows the wooden structures of Old Town Flagstaff, looking north toward the Peaks. *Library of Congress.*

When it came to Flagstaff specifically, I found this apt description in Donald Paul Shock's 1952 thesis, "A History of Flagstaff":

> *Early railroad towns were wild places. Flagstaff, in 1881, was typical of the towns that sprang up as the railroad pushed west. The residents of Flagstaff at this time were railroaders, tie choppers, gamblers and other hangers-on who followed the march of the empire. With a population of two hundred on week days, that doubled on week-ends, the town consisted of about twenty frame buildings and about an equal number of tents. A dance hall, which some called by a harder name, saloons and gambling houses operated full blast from Saturday night until Monday morning. Gun fights were common and it was usually not safe to go out after dark.[4]*

Another vivid description of the decadence found in the 1882 settlement is found in Platt Cline's book *Mountain Town*. He, in turn, quoted from Dr. Dennis Brannen's memoirs, which were printed in the July 11, 1895 edition of the *Coconino Weekly Sun*:

[Many people] *lived in tents....The town grew rapidly; that is, the saloons increased with marvelous rapidity, and religion did not spread its saving grace....Eatables and drinkables were two bits...and beer $1 per bottle....The founding of a new town...attracted a horde of desperate characters...Deadwood Dick, Wild Bill...Beefsteak Mike, Loitering Luke and others of that type....There were no regular peace officers....Lynching bees occasionally varied the monotony....At that time there were not over four [decent] women within a radius of twenty-five miles....Everyone carried weapons in open view.*[5]

Brannen continued his memoirs with specific examples of Flagstaff's quirky frontier justice:

At one trial a witness fired at the prisoner, whose life was saved by the bullet striking the buckle on his belt and glancing off. Many amusing incidents could be related of Justice Beebe's manner of dispensing justice. It is of authentic record that upon one occasion, when the testimony was somewhat tame, his honor, with his hob-nailed shoes perched awkwardly upon the bar of justice and his chair tilted back against the wall, gently dozed off into the land of dreams. He had been sleeping peacefully for half an hour when a presumptuous habituan [sic] of the court nudged him, remarking the while: "Judge, yer missin all their testimony."

The judge clapped his hand on his revolver, and pointing it at the offender's head, thundered: "You tarnal fule. I orter give yer a life sentence, but I'll give yer $50 for contempt of court." And the $50 was blown in for drinks for the crowd.

According to several accounts in the *Sun*, the courtroom was an entertaining venue. Jurors passed the bottle as they took in the proceedings, and it wasn't unusual for the judge to join in. Cline wrote about another case in which the judge halted the testimony so "we can all get a drink."

"But what about the prisoner?" a juror asked. "Why can't he have a drink too?" So all repaired to the bar, had two or three drinks, and then came back and resumed court. The prisoner was found "guilty of self defense" and acquitted.

Judge Beebe's days on the bench—colorful as they were—would come to an end. The complexion of the tiny settlement changed rapidly as it prospered and took on an air of permeance. Within a few years, the town fathers, such as they were, began discussing incorporation. Arizona was still a territory, but Flagstaff was the largest town in the northland. However, it sat inside Yavapai County and Prescott was the county seat. What that meant for those having business before the court was a long, dangerous trek down one mountain and up another to get to the courthouse. And that included those men called for jury duty, which was not an infrequent demand.

The push to create a separate county with Flagstaff as the seat began in 1884. Dr. Brannen and a former lawyer, Mickey Stewart, were elected to the territorial legislature and began garnering support for the split. Several attempts were thwarted, one by Governor Wolfley, who felt Flagstaff needed to take on more of Yavapai County's debt. This resulted in a straw-stuffed man bearing the sign "Governor Wolfey" being burned in effigy at the Flagstaff depot, much to the horror of arriving passengers. However, the push continued, backed by the good advice and financial support of the town's businessmen, and on February 19, 1891, Coconino County was officially recognized.[6]

Flagstaff's iconic red sandstone courthouse still reigns in downtown. Built in 1895, the building has two stories and a four-story tower. *Author's collection.*

The new county was huge, absorbing 70 percent of its former nemesis, Yavapai, as well as much of the Grand Canyon. It totaled 18,661 square miles, making it the second-largest county in the contiguous United States, behind San Bernadino County in California. Flagstaff paid a pretty penny for its seat in terms of assumed debt, but it gained many assets in return and the people were happy with the deal. On May 21, 1894, at what's been hailed the most important meeting in Flagstaff's history, the town unanimously endorsed incorporation; five days later, it was official. Now the work of cleaning up the streets began in earnest.

Historian Platt Cline did a great job of laying out the council's priorities in *Mountain Town*. He enumerated the ordinances that were enacted upon the people:

> *Ordinance Number One decreed that all filth and garbage must be removed to not less than a half-mile from town.....Number two banned animals roaming at large.....Number three forbade disorderly noises, brawls, fights and public drunkenness.....Number Four banned "immoderate riding, racing or driving horses through the streets."...Another called for fines of $5 to $300 for "willful and unnecessary discharge of firearms" and if not paid, jail terms.*[7]

THESE FIRST LAWS WERE aimed at corralling some of the worst behaviors— or at least the most offensive ones. They also solidified the fears of the proprietors of gambling dens, dance halls and saloons. Change was in the air and headed in their direction, and they steeled themselves for a fight.

The 1894 town council had several factions to deal with. The stability and prosperity of the lumber mill had shaped Flagstaff into a more family-centered place. There followed a sizable number of merchants and professionals who opened businesses that catered to the growing community's needs. The saloons and gambling houses, which had firmly established themselves on the southside, continued to do a brisk business. Along with the brothels, they wanted to keep operating as they always had. An especially vocal church group, however, began lobbying the new council to shut down these dens of iniquity.

Council's first attempt at appeasement was to assess fees of $15 per quarter on saloons and gambling dens and $15 a month on houses of ill repute. The marshal was given one sob story after another when he went out to collect and came back emptyhanded. Council sent him out again, with firm orders

to make the businesses pay up. The bar owners grumbled, but most ponied up their license tax. However, a boycott was called by the gamblers, who thought they were holding the winning hand over council. They closed their venues and left town for leisurely vacations, absolutely certain their customers would revolt. While some of the locals did miss playing poker and throwing dice, the end result was more business for the saloons. The owners of the gambling houses caved, one by one, and most eventually paid the $15.

The women who worked the red-light district, however, stood firm against the levy. They told the authorities they would leave Flagstaff and set up shop elsewhere, probably in nearby Williams. This stopped council, which hurriedly did a comparison of tax rates elsewhere in Arizona. It was no secret that the good women of Flagstaff were not as bothered by their menfolk visiting prostitutes as losing the family paycheck to gambling. Perhaps this was an area where the law could be more lenient. After council checked around, they agreed that $15 a month was too high a tax on the ladies and changed it to $5 a month per place. At the same time, they changed the gambling fee from $15 a game to $15 per venue. Everyone breathed a little easier except for the holy rollers, who gritted their teeth and prepared for round two.[8]

In an effort to quash the complaints from the righteous citizenry, council enacted Ordinance Number 10. According to the February 17, 1895 *Coconino Weekly Sun*:

> *Mayor Babbitt and Councilmen Daggs and Vail were present. Another ordinance was passed regulating the behavior of women of ill repute. They are no longer to be allowed to flaunt themselves and their cigarettes on the public streets and they must not enter a saloon at any time of the day or night. City Marshall [sic] George Hochderffer was instructed to strictly enforce all the provisions of this ordinance.*

Above: The outside of the historic Paseo del Norte, which now houses various businesses on South San Francisco Street. *Author's collection.*

Opposite: A view inside Paseo del Norte. This building was once a brothel, evidenced by the many small rooms off the upstairs hallway. *Author's collection.*

A view down Flagstaff's South San Francisco Street. This area was known as the red-light district in the 1890s but is now being gentrified. *Author's collection*.

This did little to appease the saintly protesters, who objected to lowering the taxes on the sinful delights of the southside. They continued to grumble and kept a principled eye on law enforcement, all the while attempting to recruit more citizens to their cause.

A few months later, the new ordinance was tested when two women were arrested by Marshall Hochderffer for singing in a saloon. They hired an attorney who argued to the court that the town had no right preventing his clients from pursuing their legitimate occupations. The *Sun* weighed in on the side of polite society while the judge initially wavered but then found them guilty. One of the women, Agnes Nelson, filed an appeal and continued singing for saloon owner Donahue. In the meantime, council thought better of their overstep and amended the ordinance adding that it was "not construed to prevent any female from playing musical instruments or singing in any (legal) saloon."

A year and a half later, the issue was raised again, and this time the Catholics had joined the opposition. With the help of local lumberman Michael Riordan, who had once studied to be a Jesuit priest, the tax on female singers was increased from $10 per woman per month to $55. This was quite high, and many of the smaller taverns folded. The saloon singers, who beguiled the male patrons and kept them at the bar drinking, were an effective target. They appeared to be more unpopular than actual prostitutes, as their clientele spent household money whiling away the evenings. However, the reformers were not through yet.

On August 1, 1897, a fee of $500 per month per female singer was levied against the saloons, payable in advance. This appeared to be the stake through the heart of prostitution, gambling and carousing in Flagstaff. But was it? The ladies in red were still selling their wares, the bars that still stood were open all hours of the day and night and gambling houses were plentiful. So it was back to court, where a ban on "bawdy houses" was passed, under the guise of fire dangers, and the taxes on saloons and gambling halls were again raised.

By this time, a sizable portion of the citizenry had tired of the constant moral outrage and legal maneuverings of the righteous few. It was Thomas E. Pollock, an Iowa transplant and entrepreneur, who came up with a solution. Elected mayor in 1901, he designated a few half blocks south of the tracks as Flagstaff's red-light district. It was agreed that the marshal would not enforce the restrictive ordinances in this area, and bawdy houses, saloons and gambling were allowed to exist therein.

Throughout the turbulent years of forming and reforming the town, it was evident that several groups held different visions for the community. That they were able to hammer them out and coexist afterward says more about the town than the number of its churches and saloons. While gambling was a sore spot that would reappear periodically, and Flagstaff, like other towns, was affected by Prohibition, the people here started the twentieth century generally satisfied with their piece of mountain.

COMMODORE PERRY OWENS

Known as a deadly shot, and recently dubbed the "Fabulous Fabio of the Wild West," Commodore Perry Owens was one interesting cowboy. Part Daniel Boone, part Wyatt Earp—and a huge helping of Jesse James mixed in—Owens's life straddled the shifting times of the late 1800s. His story is fascinating and enmeshed in the down-and-dirty wickedness that ran rampant in northern Arizona. These were confusing times, when it wasn't easy to tell the good guys from the bad and frontier justice was widely accepted. Owen's life reflects how complicated and wild the West really was in the late nineteenth century. He was an outlaw, a lawman, a hero and a villain. While Commodore is buried in Flagstaff's Citizens Cemetery, his adventures largely took place in Apache County to the east and Yavapai to the west.[9]

Owens was born on July 29, 1852, in Hawkins County, Tennessee, the fifth in a family of seven children. His father was christened Oliver H. Perry Owens in honor of the American naval commander Oliver Perry. Commodore was named by his mother, Fanny Owens, and the young boy was said to have been close to her. However, many biographers indicate he was frequently at odds with his father, an abusive and difficult man. Whether or not this is true, Commodore left home around age fourteen and ran west toward Oklahoma. It's believed he first worked for the railroad as a buffalo hunter, killing the beasts for meat to feed the workers. He refined his shooting skills and was ambidextrous when it came to firearms. Later, he found work as a cowboy, moving from one ranch to another and leading an outlaw's

This iconic image of Commodore Perry Owens was taken before he was elected sheriff of Navajo County. He had quite a head of hair! *Wikipedia.*

life on the side. In a later interview, Owens claimed he "ran with a gang of tough characters" back then and was involved in smuggling whiskey and rustling.

By the time he was thirty, Commodore had ventured further west into Arizona. He had a knack with horses and was the ranch foreman for James Houck and A.E. Hennings in Navajo Springs. Owens homesteaded a ranch nearby and soon found himself embroiled in the growing tensions that pervaded Apache County. This was the northeast part of the Arizona Territory, which eventually extended south almost as far as Tucson. In the mid- to late 1800s, Apache County was a hotbed of cattle rustling, gambling, fighting and thievery. There was so much ill will between the various factions that it's hard to keep straight who was in charge when and of what. It bears taking a closer look at this microcosm of the Wild West in order to understand the people who lived here.

After the Civil War and with the building of the Atlantic Pacific Railways, interest was piqued in the relatively unexplored western territories. In northern Arizona, the lands had been occupied for centuries by Native American tribes, notably the Navajo, Hopi and Apache. The Anglo ranchers and sheepherders who settled the area came around the 1860s. There are many reports of skirmishes and ill will between the Native Americans and early settlers, but there's also evidence of cooperation. After the war, as military men and Indian agents began appearing in town, suspicion grew among the old-timers and the tribespeople. Simply put, they had developed their own ways of dealing with one another and with settling disagreements.

Few were happy to see the "lawmen" from Washington arriving. Add to this mix an alarming and dangerous new faction—cattle rustlers and horse thieves, who were on the run and sought refuge in Apache County. These outlaws didn't change their ways when they resettled; many set up new rustling schemes and were known for terrorizing the peaceful towns of St. Johns and Snowflake. Finally, there were the monied easterners whose very interest in exploiting the area was the oil poured on the brewing fires. Apache County became a violent, unpredictable territory in which neighbor turned against neighbor and mistrust was everywhere. Commodore Owens arrived at this hornet's nest around 1882 to work and homestead his piece of paradise.

Although his reputation as a deadly shot preceded him, Owens had his hands full fending off rustlers at Navajo Springs. During this time, another aspect of his nature—a colder and more violent one—became apparent. The Houck-Hennings ranch was a frequent target of horse thieves, some of whom were the nearby Navajos. It's said Owens killed at least two Native men he caught either stealing horses or attacking the stage line. He was dubbed "Iron Man" by both the Navajos and the townspeople for his no-nonsense approach to theft. Today one finds that there is an air of mythology surrounding Owens's life. While some of the stories are witnessed accounts, newspapers of the day don't always agree on the facts. One incident from 1883 has Owens arrested for killing a young Navajo boy near the ranch whom he'd accused of thievery.

Denis Riordan, future Flagstaff mill owner and elder brother to Tim and Michael, was a respected Indian agent at the time. He was notified that an Anglo man had shot and killed an unarmed youth at Navajo Springs. While tragic in any event, it was especially upsetting as the thirteen-year-old was the son of Chief Begay. The boy lived long enough to identify his killer as C.P. Owens and swore that he was doing nothing wrong when shot. Riordan and Lieutenant Lockett of the Fourth Cavalry launched an investigation, following the shooter's tracks to the Houck's ranch house. There they confronted Owens, who claimed he caught the boy stealing one of Houck's steeds and admitted shooting him. Riordan arrested Commodore and took him to Fort Wingate, where he awaited trial on the charge of murder.

Riordan wrote a report of the arrest in which he said that the two men, Owens and Houck, were a danger to the overall peace of Apache County. Riordan claimed that twenty-five Indians were shot at by the two, including an Indian woman. The Indian agent went on to voice his concerns about retribution. He was fearful of being ambushed by either man as revenge for turning Owens in. Denis Riordan was certain a jury would not convict the gunslinger, and he was right. The case went to trial and Commodore Owens was acquitted by an Apache County jury. The truth was, plenty of men despised the Navajo as much as they did the horse thieves and the newly minted peace officers from back East. A marksman like C.P. Owens, who'd stand up to any troublemaker and had ice in his trigger finger, was an asset. A contingency of cattlemen who'd suffered tremendous losses to both the rustlers and the Native Americans convinced Owens to run for sheriff in the 1886 election. He accepted the challenge and defeated the opposition, starting his two-year term in January 1887.[10]

Immediately upon assuming office, Commodore was entrusted with sixteen bench warrants left unserved by his predecessor. At the time, Apache County was a stunning 21,177 square miles, larger than New Hampshire and Vermont combined. Owens set out to bring in the named perpetrators and, if they resisted, had few qualms about killing them. The men he deputized appeared to be of the same persuasion. It's said that over half the sixteen were found dead with the indictment on their chest, weighted down by a rock. How much of this is bravado and myth is debatable. What's certain is that Sheriff Owens's term in office was filled with so much bloodshed and violence that decent folk hid in their homes. Surprisingly, the end result was a cleaned-up county—one that was safer and more law-abiding than it had been in decades. It was the getting there that had newspapers and councilmen wringing their hands.

The most defining day (some would say infamous) of Sheriff Owens's term was Sunday, September 4, 1887. He was in Holbrook, Arizona, ostensibly to gather a jury pool. However, it was known to him that Andy Blevins, aka Andy Cooper, had returned to the town and was presently residing in one of his mother's homes. Blevins was part of the Texas Blevins Brothers, a notorious gang of outlaws who escaped to Arizona to avoid arrest for rustling and murder. Like so many others, they continued their rampaging here. The Blevins were part of the bloodiest range conflict of its time, the Pleasant Valley War. While the subject of several books on its own, simply put, the war was between two feuding families, the Grahams and the Tewksburys. It involved grazing rights and boundaries and cattlemen versus sheepherders. Many other families were pulled into the conflict, including hired guns, the Hashknife Outfit, the Daggs and various lawmen. Commodore Owens had managed to steer clear of publicly supporting one side or the other during his term as sheriff.

The old Blevins home is the notorious site of the Holbrook shootout involving Owens and Andy Cooper-Blevins. Today it serves as the Holbrook Senior Citizens Center. *Author's collection.*

That September morning, Cooper-Blevins had been boasting of his murderous escapades, saying he'd killed John Tewksbury and Bill Jacobs two days earlier. He'd also let it be known that he wasn't afraid of the law; on the contrary, the law was afraid of him. Owens had been catching heat for not bringing Andy Blevins in. The man was a murderous thief and a threat to decent people all over the county. There had also been rumors that Owens and Blevins were friends and Commodore was cutting Andy some slack. Whether it was the insinuations of cowardice or the editorials calling for his badge, Owens was moved to action that day. The sheriff approached the Blevins house around four o'clock in the afternoon. He was fully armed and carried a warrant issued on Blevins from the year before, charging him with horse theft.

Owens had his Winchester rifle in arm as he stepped up onto the front porch. As always, his six-shooter was on his hip, stock facing forward. There were twelve people inside the four-room casa, including six females and two infants. There were two front doors off the porch, one on the east end and the other at the far west. Sheriff Owens knocked at the east front door and called to Cooper-Blevins to come outside. Eyewitnesses claimed Andy came to the east door, opened it a crack and greeted Commodore. Some claimed his pistol was unholstered. His brother John stood by at the west door.

> *Owens said, "I have a warrant for you, and I want you to come with me." Cooper replied, "What warrant is it Owens?" The Sheriff answered, "The warrant for stealing horses." Cooper wanted to think for a few minutes and Owens said, "Are you ready?" and was answered by Cooper, "In a few minutes." Owens said, "No, right away," then fired the ball from his Winchester striking Cooper in the center of the abdomen, passing through the bowels and coming out near the spine.*

As Andy Cooper fell backward into the house, his brother John pushed open the west door and fired at Commodore. He missed but killed a horse tied to a tree. The sheriff jumped back while reloading his rifle, pivoted and fired a shot into John Blevins's shoulder, effectively disarming him. Owens then backed off the front porch, taking another shot at Cooper-Blevins, grazing the dying man's arm.

As Commodore stood across the street at the blacksmith shop, another man inside the house, Mote Roberts, decided to make his escape. He had been sitting at a table when the shooting began, so he crept into a bedroom in the back. Roberts then jumped from the bedroom window, six-shooter in hand. As he turned toward the northeast corner of the house, he was hit in the shoulder by Owens's fourth shot. The ball struck Roberts from behind and passed through his left lung, shattering his collarbone. The poor man crawled back into the house through the back door and bled to death on the kitchen floor.

Sadly, the afternoon's bloodshed wasn't over yet. As Owens stood reloading his rifle, the front door burst open and fifteen-year-old Sam Blevins ran out, brandishing Andy's six-shooter. The boy's mother was right behind him, desperately trying to restrain him and pull her son inside. Sam, however, was wild with grief and rage, and when he caught sight of Commodore across the way, he began to raise the weapon. With the same deadly aim that had taken down the others, Owens raised his rifle and fired. The boy fell down at his mother's feet, his head inside the door she'd tried vainly to pull him back through. With that, the sheriff turned and made his way into town to file his report. He passed a man on the road who yelled, "Did you get them all?" Owens famously answered, "I know I have. Whenever I draw a bead and shoot, I know I have something."

Top: Commodore Owens's Seligman house. *Author's collection.*

Bottom: Owens's former home and saloon sit on a corner in Seligman, Arizona, with a small museum on the premises. *Author's collection.*

Commodore Owens received a lot of criticism over the carnage that resulted from that day. He faced three separate coroner's juries and was acquitted in each, his actions found justified. Andy Blevins was a terrorist, and all but his family heaved a sigh of relief that he was dead. However, Mote Roberts and Sam Blevins were a different story. There were some who said Roberts was unarmed when Owens shot him. The coroner cast doubt on that accusation, but the whispers continued. Young Sam's death was the one that garnered the most outrage. The scenario was tragic, with the boy dying as his mother cradled his small body. Owens later said he suffered great remorse over killing the boy, but that a child with a loaded gun could kill him just as easily as a seasoned outlaw.[11]

Owens ran for sheriff again in 1888, but he lost. He was never elected to the office again, although years later he was appointed temporary sheriff of Navajo County. The rest of his term was quiet, and after it was over, he went back to his ranch near Navajo Springs. He was known for raising prize stallion and also served as a guard for the Atlantic-Pacific Railroad. Owens was occasionally asked to ride with a posse, which he gladly did.

Commodore Owens's grave is marked by a simple headstone and chain-linked slab. He's buried on a gentle rise in Citizens Cemetery. *Author's collection.*

At some point, Owens moved farther west to Seligman, Arizona. In 1902, he married Elizabeth Jane Barrett, and the two ran a saloon and general store in the town. They had no children and, in later years, would take the train to California and stay for a time. On May 28, 1919, Owens died in Seligman of Bright's Disease at age sixty-seven. Platt Cline reached out to Commodore's widow to ask why the former sheriff was buried in Coconino County. Elizabeth Owens responded that her husband had wanted to be buried in Seligman, near his beloved home; however, she felt his gravesite would be better looked after in Flagstaff. His remains are safely interred in the historic Citizens Cemetery, on the crest of a gentle knoll.[12]

Thus ends the complicated story of Commodore Perry Owens, a man loved by some and feared by most, who lived life on his own terms. By all accounts, he had softened in his later years, expressing sadness over a few of the deaths that came at his hand. There's no doubt but that Owens was elected to "clean up the county" for those who either lacked the skill or the bravery to do it themselves. He fulfilled that duty when those before him failed, and Apache County was a safer place to live after his term. He was a legend and a myth, but he was also a man who lived through the taming of the Wild West and played his part as best he knew how.

BURYING THE DEAD

lagstaff is home to two historic cemeteries, both situated on the south side of town and both adjacent to the Northern Arizona University campus. Citizens Cemetery, the older and more eclectic of the two, sits across San Francisco Street from various NAU classrooms and parking areas. Its southern border is eerily close to student housing, with metal fencing separating it from campus life. Calvary Cemetery, owned by the Catholic Diocese, lies slightly west and to the south of Citizens, less than a mile as the crow flies. Long ago it bordered the southern edge of the NAU campus; today it's almost in the middle of the bustling university. Stroll through either place on an afternoon outing and you'll find familiar names on weathered gravestones. Both cemeteries are active, with burials taking place weekly among the pine-treed grounds and rolling hills. Of course, Flagstaff's cemeteries weren't always shrouded in peace and beauty. Darkness and superstition often surrounded the burying of the dead, and there were rumored dirty dealings, sometimes involving money exchanged, in the past.[13]

Greenwood was the town's first official cemetery, Flagstaff's "Boot Hill" as it were. The grounds were located at the base of Mars Hill, where Thorpe Park sits today. Greenwood was the repository for many an unknown outlaw. It was also close to the town's "hanging tree," so dubbed when nine bodies were found strung up in its branches one morning in the mid-1880s. This presents several questions: Which tree was it, truly? Where was it located? Was there, perhaps, more than one? A trip down the rabbit hole is called for.

The western edge of today's Thorpe Park holds the remains of some former Boot Hill residents. Behind the sign is the road leading up to Lowell Observatory. *Author's collection.*

In his book *They Came to the Mountain*, Platt Cline has a picture of the notorious old pine, circa 1930. The caption beneath states:

> *Flagstaff's "hanging tree" on which the bodies of nine outlaws were found hanging by their necks one morning in the mid-eighties, after a night's work by a local vigilante committee. The tree stood near the west end of Cherry Street in what is now City Park.*

The men hanging there were said to be troublemakers who had "plagued the community for months." They were gamblers, thieves, rustlers and cheats, and local officials had been unable to rein them in. A group of vigilante citizens decided they'd had enough and, that night, quietly set about bringing the outlaws to heel.[14]

Other historians have placed the tree several blocks east, closer to today's downtown library. As noted earlier, more than one pine might have been called into service for these occasions. Lynching parties were not as uncommon in the 1880s as the town would like to believe. While nowhere near as trigger-happy as Prescott and Tucson, Flag had its share of street fighting and frontier justice. The sturdy pine near today's library was closer to the old jail, and several news articles noted the short distance that a doomed prisoner had to walk to his execution.

Whether the old hanging tree was one or several, its victims were eventually cut down and buried in Greenwood Cemetery. According to historian Joseph Meehan, there were about one hundred grave sites inside its perimeter. However, in 1891, respectable community groups chipped in to buy forty acres south of town for use as burial grounds. This was the beginning of Citizens Cemetery, and it was supported by the Masons, the Odd Fellows, the veterans and other groups. By 1900, the community had been barred from using Greenwood, which raised the question of what to do with bodies buried there.[15]

I want to digress for a paragraph to speculate on a situation I've found interesting. Greenwood Cemetery—and possibly the old hanging tree— sat at the base of what became known as Mars Hill. This is the mesa on which Percival Lowell built his esteemed observatory. The town of Flagstaff lobbied Dr. Lowell and his team mightily to locate it here, and in 1894 he agreed. The effect that Lowell Observatory has had on the town should not be minimized; it's attracted international attention and scholars from around the world. In the late 1890s, an impressive road to access the observatory was carved into the hill, a seriously steep switchback that's still used today as the main entrance. And what did every visitor, every astronomer and every out-of-town guest have to pass as they began the ascent? Greenwood Cemetery and the gnarled old pine trees and dirt mounds that littered the grounds. While I've found nothing in Cline's books or the *Sun* to support my theory, I've often thought the move to Citizens was hastened by Dr. Lowell and his elite entourage's arrival.

Back to the story, and this is a good one. It was in autumn of 1914 that the town council decided it was time to move all the remains from Greenwood over to Citizens. J. Vishno, a teamster, was hired to disinter the bodies and cart them over to their new resting place. According to Cline:

> *As Vishno and helpers dug and loaded bones and other remains into burlap bags for removal, fascinated observers were two ten-year-old lads, Pete Michelbach and Ernie Yost, who ignored orders from parents to stay away because of the danger of contagion. Pete said, more than 70 years later, that he had never forgotten seeing part of a little girl's dress turned up.…He added that Vishno kept himself fumigated, both*

internally and externally, with bourbon whiskey…sipping and dousing himself frequently.[16]

The pay was good, $8.00 per grave and an extra $1.50 for moving the gravestone. However, the men moved only forty graves, and an official 1904 count showed a total of sixty-four graves in Greenwood. Several historians believe even more bodies were unaccounted for, given the poor recordkeeping

The front gate into Citizens Cemetery is open during daylight hours to the public. The grounds contain many historic graves. *Author's collection.*

and transient nature of the 1880s. So, at a minimum, twenty-four bodies remain interred in Thorpe Park today, most likely under the tennis courts.

Our story now moves along to Citizens Cemetery, the final resting place for several of the early settlers mentioned in this book. It's iconic iron gate opens at eight o'clock each morning and swings shut at sunset. Visitors are welcomed to roam the forty acres as long as they are respectful of the residents' graves. While there's definitely some mingling of the eras, one begins to intuit the various sections by the different markers and inscriptions. The Masonic grounds are located in the far south acreage, an immediate right inside the front gate and down a dirt road. Potter's Field is a straight walk east on Buttercup Avenue and then off to the left, just below the cemetery's offices. The military burials are easily identified by the small flags adorning the graves and are in the southeast corner of Citizens. In my wanderings through these peaceful, historic grounds I've discovered two areas where markers indicate infants and young children. Scattered throughout the forty acres are several large family plots, with names most locals would recognize.

Just who are some of Citizens' most notorious residents? I'll start with one of the saddest sites, a nondescript raised rectangle—a double plot— that holds the remains of Marie Walkup and her four children. Their tragic demise was the subject of my first book for The History Press, *Flagstaff's Walkup Family Murders*. While difficult to condense, the story revolves around a well-known, middle-class family in the 1930s. The head of the house, J.D. Walkup, was active in local politics and well-placed to pursue even higher office. His wife, Marie, was essentially invisible. The biggest impression she left on the town was killing her four children as they slept and then driving north to the Flagstaff Country Club, where she shot herself. Whether she was in the throes of depression or angry at a perceived slight is unknown. J.D. was in Phoenix at the time, and when he received a call from the sheriff to return, he faced the sad task of burying his family. They are interred in the cemetery's Masonic section, with Daniel, Rose, John and Elizabeth buried side by side. Marie was buried at the head of the plot and at an angle to her children. At one time a large tree bisected the grave, separating the mother from her offspring. It has since been cut down and the stump removed. In the last few years, visitors have begun placing decorative rocks and small toys at the grave site.[17]

Another resident of the cemetery is a man who was iconic in his day yet is now a virtual unknown. James Vail was a wealthy entrepreneur who came to Flag around 1882 when he was twenty-one. He eventually owned

Above: This interesting historic gravestone marks the plot of George Prime in Flagstaff's Citizens Cemetery. *Author's collection*.

Opposite: The Walkup family grave site is nondescript and located in the Masonic section. Visitors have left painted rocks, pinwheels and toys there. *Author's collection*.

a cattle ranch, a saloon and restaurant on Railroad Avenue, and various other properties in town. He served on Flagstaff's first council in 1894. Vail's name was frequently mentioned when the "blue laws" were being hammered out. His restaurant and saloon were located where today's Crystal Magic stands, and much of the foundation is original to Vail. As councilman, he voted for higher taxes and more restrictions on bars serving alcohol. His establishment, the Parlor Saloon, was

considered "respectable" but would presumably have been subject to the same new laws. Regardless, he was a popular figure in town at the dawn of the twentieth century. Sadly, Vail was involved in a carriage accident that left him crippled and in constant pain. Although he sought help from doctors in California, little could be done to improve his condition. On April 3, 1906, Vail went into the empty barn on his property and shot himself in the head. His wife and children mourned his passing, as did much of Flagstaff—many establishments closed the day of his funeral.[18]

As mentioned before, several of the subjects in this book are interred in Citizens. Commodore Perry Owen's grave is catty-corner from the TWA memorial. Both sit near the crest of a gentle knoll, just south of the cemetery's offices. Another grave in that general area is tainted with wickedness, although not by its inhabitant. Jay Lively was a healthy, active seventeen-year-old-boy when he was tragically struck down in March 1984. He was returning home from hockey practice in Tempe that evening, driving north on Interstate 17. A woman pulling a horse trailer was headed south in the northbound lane and plowed into Lively's vehicle, hitting several other cars as well. Seven people were killed in the carnage, although the woman, who was intoxicated, lived. The Lively family lobbied furiously for the driver to be charged with vehicular homicide and be given a lengthy sentence:

Today, the laws are far more strict, due in-part to this tragic accident. For a long time, Jerry Lively said he was bitter over the death of his son. "You're never the same; it takes all your dreams and hopes and blows them out the window." Through the years, he has softened his views somewhat. "I've come to terms with it," he said. "You learn to live with life. And, we were blessed with two beautiful daughters."

The driver served all of her seven-plus-year sentence, which was the most the judge could impose at the time. The City of Flagstaff renamed its indoor ice rink in the young teen's honor, and the Jay Lively Activity Center is a mainstay for indoor hockey and recreational skating.[19]

Ben Doney, the forgotten namesake of Doney Park, is buried in one of the veterans' sections. It would be a step too far to call Doney "wicked," but he was a pain in the behind during his time here. He served as mayor in 1909, but it was a short term. He and several council members tried to reverse course on restricting the red-light district, lobbying to remove all taxes from the saloons and "cathouses." There were some in town who agreed with the move but more who disapproved. However, when Doney made noise about overthrowing Lowell Observatory, complaining that the town had illegally given Dr. Lowell the land atop of Mars Hill, he and his two cohorts were "unelected." That was not the end of Ben Doney though—far from it. His name appeared frequently in the *Coconino Sun*, complaining about the city's corruption or defending himself against various accusations. He died in October 1933, falling in the snow and hitting his head on a wagon wheel. Ben Doney was a character, a cranky old man who was a burr in whatever council was seated at the time. Yet the old pioneer was sorely missed and roundly feted when he passed at eighty-nine.[20]

Leaving Citizens and moving south, one passes beneath an elegant yet weathered wrought-iron arch to enter Calvary Catholic Cemetery. Smaller than the other grounds by half, Calvary is just as peaceful with its manicured grounds, apple trees and pines. An unobstructed view of the majestic San Francisco Peaks can be found on a clear day. *Enchanting* might be a strange word to describe a cemetery, but it's applicable here. The arch over its main entry reads: CALVARY CEMETERY, 1892. However, there is another, older entrance with a story attached, which I'll get to later.

In 1887, as Flagstaff continued to grow and became more settled, a group of Catholics met to discuss the need for a church and a priest. Both the Riordans and the Babbitts were Catholic, so there was momentum behind the movement. Michael Riordan was elected to lead the charge, and he wrote to the bishop, asking permission to fundraise for a building. The bishop gave his permission but added that he had no priest to send here. There were visiting priests in the late 1800s, and many Catholic homes had their own chapel. Not having a priest immediately available did not deter the group. Riordan's initiative got the ball rolling, and the Church of the Nativity was built in time to hold Christmas services in 1888. Establishing a Catholic cemetery naturally followed the opening of the church, and Calvary was chartered in 1892. Matt Riordan furthered the cause by deeding ten acres of land to the diocese to be used for the cemetery in 1897.[21]

Calvary Catholic Cemetery has many religious statues and grottos situated within its rolling grounds. *Author's collection.*

There are several family burial sites nestled among the trees here, with familiar surnames within the community. The Babbitts and the Riordans have large, multigenerational plots that are situated close to one another. Interestingly, given both families' prominence, neither is especially ornate. Another large pioneer family, the Michelbachs, are buried here, as are the Fronskes and Zanzucchis. The Nackards have a lovely area on the south end of the cemetery, close to where the original gate was located. The story about that entryway involves the Riordans' lumber mill and the many Hispanic workers employed there.

The Arizona Lumber and Timber Company built housing for its employees in an area close by the yard. This area became a town of sorts with a store, a hospital and small homes, many of which were closer to being shacks. It became known as Los Chantes, or Shack Row. At the south end of Los Chantes, the lumber company placed a statue known as Santo, the Sacred Heart of Jesus. The Hispanic people believed He would bless and protect their neighborhood, especially from the spirit of La Llorona. La Llorona, sometimes called the wailing woman, is the spirit of a mother who drowned her children out of vengeance against her husband. Her spirit is still said to roam the night, calling for her children—or any children—to follow her.

When Los Chantes was shut down, the statue was ceremoniously moved to Calvary Cemetery and placed inside the front gate. However, vandals and thoughtless pranksters continuously broke Santo's outstretched arms until the caregivers finally had the arms re-sculpted to lay closer to the statue's torso. The gate itself is no longer the main entrance, but that area retains a historic aura with its interesting grottos and ornate grave markers.

John Hawks is another resident of Calvary Cemetery. Hawks was a well-liked entrepreneur, one of the area's first settlers when it was still known as Antelope Park. However, it's the fate of two of his sons, George and Will, that's of interest here. That the brothers were buried apart from the rest of the family was the result of a bar fight that got out of hand. The incident happened on January 18, 1887, and it shook the town to its core. In the early morning hours, local cowboy William Lamb was drunk and singing loudly in Berry's saloon. George Hawks, a bit of a

Father Vabre was a Catholic priest who was deeply loved by the community he served. He's buried at Calvary alongside fellow clergymen. *Author's collection.*

hothead who liked his guns, told Lamb to shut up. The singing sot was angered by Hawk's rude command, but he went outside and cooled off. Soon, though, Lamb returned and took up his offensive yodeling, this time even louder. George's younger brother, William Hawks, gave George a pistol and told him if he didn't use it on Lamb then William would "give it" to George.

At that point, Lamb started walking toward the door. George Hawks ran after him and attacked him from behind, pistol-whipping Lamb about the head. Confusion reigned, and the proprietor, John Berry, jumped in to wrestle the gun away from George. A shot rang out, and Berry cried in pain as he slumped to the floor. The two Hawks brothers made a dash out the door and ran down the alley. Berry lingered for a day before dying a painful, agonizing death.

There were few places to hide in 1887, and the Hawks brothers were soon arrested and taken to the old jail. The building wasn't the sturdiest or the safest, so two men stood guard that night. Sometime around 1:00 a.m. they noticed an angry mob turning the corner, headed toward the jail. All of the men were masked, and two of them trained their guns on the frightened pair, ordering them to step aside or face the consequences. The hapless guards did as they were told, dropping their weapons and offering no resistance. Some of the masked men entered the jail, and shortly afterward pleas were heard, followed by gunfire. The mob dispersed, and both Hawks brothers were found dead inside their cell from gunshots. A noose lay coiled on the floor, presumably at the ready if the bullets failed. Interestingly, the two guards and one other man were charged in the Hawkses' deaths, but after the accused posted bond, the case disappeared.

As said before, the killing and the lynching deeply affected the small town. Most people had hoped the days of gunslinging and vigilante justice were over. All four men were well known in Flagstaff, but only Berry was well liked. The community still regarded Papa Hawks as a good man and didn't hold his offspring's actions against him. His sons are said to buried somewhere on what is now NAU's North Campus.[22]

The last story from Calvary Cemetery (although there are so many more!) is of young Leo Bart. Once again, Leo was by no means wicked; in fact, he was a hardworking, well-liked young man in town. Any wickedness comes from the times and circumstances that were part of 1900s Flagstaff. The *Coconino Sun* ran a lengthy obituary for Bart, which was unusual for a twenty-two-year-old of no special stature. However, Leo was the sole support of his mother and sisters, and he stepped up after his father's untimely death to take care of them.

Leo Bart was born in Canada and came with his family to Flagstaff in 1898. He completed his schooling here and started working at the Arizona Lumber & Timber Company. However, his dream—like that of so many other young men—was to work for the railroad. He was hired by the Atchison, Topeka and Santa Fe and was working as a brakeman at the time of the accident. The following is from the *Sun*:

> *There were no witnesses. The train slowed down to enter the east switch at Canyon Diablo about 9:45 Monday night, to allow passenger (train) No. 10 from the west to pass. Leo was last seen by the conductor on the*

running board, midway between cab and engine, with a lighted lantern in his hand. It was his business as brakeman to throw open the switch and he had gone forth to do so. The train came to a standstill within about two car lengths of the switch opening and the conductor stepped to the ground. The switch had not been opened—and the light carried by Leo Bart was not in evidence.

A few moments later the trainmen found the body lying in the center of the track and the severed head nearby on the north side of the track. The work had been terribly done—but instantly. The news flashed over the wire to the Bart home where it caused the fond mother and affectionate sisters such unspeakable grief as can only be vaguely comprehended.

Many men lost lives and limbs while working the railroad. Leo Bart's death had all the markings of a tragic accident, but others were linked to outside pressures and carelessness. Working for the railroad paid well and carried prestige and romance, but it was a dangerous job.[23]

At the beginning of this chapter, I allude to "darkness" and "rumors" surrounding the two historic cemeteries. That's really not surprising, given that they *are* cemeteries. The most insidious tales involve the removal of bodies, but I've found nothing at all to support such claims. Because many of those who lie beneath the hallow, rolling grounds led checkered lives, it's also not surprising a few ghost stories have sprung up around them. A number of these are told by students, who either lived in a dorm nearby or took an illicit midnight stroll through the graveyards. I'm going to share a story from each place, starting with Calvary.

NAU's McConnell Hall is rumored to be built on the graves of the departed who once resided across the street in Calvary Cemetery. As far as I can tell, this is patently false. Yes, the Catholic Church owned the land the hall now sits on but sold it to the university in the 1970s. In any event, McConnell is reportedly the most haunted building on campus, with stories of disappearing specters roaming its halls, music that floats through the air without a source, water turning on and off and the sound of children giggling in the nighttime. It's said that an obsessive-compulsive architect designed the hall so that each room received six minutes of sunlight a day. After completing the job, the man was checking his work and found that one room did not receive the requisite six minutes. The architect became so distraught he killed himself in that room, and many of the noises and eerie feelings emanate from that wing.

Citizens Cemetery also has its stories, some revolving around spirits that walk at night. The following story centers on the Walkup family and goes like this: A young woman brought a decorative flower to the grave, which is situated about two feet from a large tree. She said that as she sat on the raised wooden tie that defines the site, a large black bird flew to the tree and sat on a limb. The woman said that the bird "gave me the creeps." She had an uncomfortable feeling the raven was watching her. That night, after she went to bed, she was awakened by a dark, heavy presence in her room. She was certain she had been "visited" by the spirit of someone, and she felt that the someone was Marie Walkup.

DECEIVING THE TERRITORIAL ASSEMBLY

*B*y the late 1890s, it appeared a growing number of Flagstaffians were happy that an arduous mountain trek separated them from their fellow Arizonans. The small town had begun to carve out its own identity as a family-friendly place—a people who wooed Percival Lowell and his observatory and firmly pushed the saloons and dance halls south of the tracks. The fact that the lumber mill was operating full force and employed hundreds of ordinary men contributed to Flagstaff's whiff of superiority over Phoenix and Tucson. Life was often dangerous in the untamed lands south of here. The town's first councils as well as the businessmen and ranchers worked hard to keep its growth on a stable track.

I'm going to ask the reader to forgive me as I digress yet again. I've been accused of painting too rosy a picture of Flag's early settlers and "town fathers." I'll plead guilty to the charge, but there is an explanation that's grounded in historic writings and interviews. Yes, the first councils were composed of white men, but after 1914, women's names began to appear with increasing regularity as county treasurer, recorder and superintendent of schools. Some were trailblazers themselves. Mary Costigan, who in the 1920s managed the Orpheum Theatre, was the first woman in the nation to possess a broadcasting license. Hispanic families have also been an important part of Flagstaff's community, even if not politically prominent in the early years. Flagstaff wasn't a melting pot; however, the first settlers were *all* from some other part of the country. We know Native American tribes roamed northern Arizona long before Thomas McMillian arrived, but none I'm aware of were chased out of Old Town in the 1890s.[24]

I write this to emphasize a nebulous theme that I've found throughout Flagstaff's early history. Many railroad towns went bust after the initial boom of excitement that the industry brought in faded. While Flag had the benefit of its natural resources, it was also blessed by the fortitude of its early leaders. These people were determined to grow a town at the base of the San Francisco Peaks. Some of the families, such as the Babbitts of Cincinnati and the Riordans of Chicago, came from monied backgrounds and were quite educated. Thomas McMillian, the area's first white settler, was well traveled and the nephew of President James Polk's wife. None of these people were rubes. They also had a vision for this mountain town and skillfully navigated a path forward. That

Governor Wolfley was as unpopular with all of Arizona as he was in Flagstaff. He barely served sixteen months in office. *M. Bell, photographer. Gov. Wolfley, Arizona., circa 1916. Library of Congress.*

Flagstaff was seen as an anomaly by much of Arizona's territorial assembly was just one more needle to thread. The story behind Northern Arizona University's inception does a good job of illustrating this point.[25]

The story begins in late 1884, when the move was on to split a new county, the future Coconino, off from the then sprawling Yavapai County. People in Flagstaff were weary of the tedious and sometimes dangerous trek to Prescott, whether to conduct county business or serve in a jury pool. Dr. Brannen was tapped to represent the town, and he gathered huge support for the change. A bill was introduced at the Fourteenth Arizona Territorial Assembly, which convened in Prescott in January 1887 and ran through March 10, 1887. Assemblyman W.H. Ashurst presented the proposal, named the Frisco County bill, but it was defeated by one vote. Undeterred, Flagstaff elected several ranchers from Yavapai, who were sympathetic to the split, to the House of Representatives. Michael Riordan renamed the bill the "Coconino County" bill, and it was brought before the Fifteenth Arizona Territorial Legislature.

The Fifteenth Assembly started in Prescott on January 21, 1889, but moved to Phoenix on February 7. It did not adjourn until April 11, 1889, earning it the name of the "Hold-over Legislature." This was a contentious assembly from the start. Governor C. Meyer Zulick was unpopular and held his position only because of a friendship with President Cleveland. It was assumed Zulick would lose his governorship when Benjamin Harrison ascended to the presidency on March 4, 1889. One of the biggest issues the assembly faced was the vote on relocating Arizona's capital from Prescott to Phoenix. Governor Zulick held his office long enough to see the bill pass and then the session was suspended while the assembly was moved south. People in Phoenix had the foresight to erect a large, new capitol building and it was finished just in time to accommodate the officials. The legislature reconvened in Phoenix on February 7, 1889, and business resumed until time for official appointments. The Republican majority did not want to confirm Zulick's duly appointed nominees, again certain Zulick would be replaced when President-elect Harrison was inaugurated. This was indeed the case; Harrison nominated Lewis Wolfley as Arizona's governor, and the U.S. Senate confirmed him on March 28. Wolfley had his own list of nominees for territorial positions, which the council quickly approved. The result was that, for almost a year's time, Arizona had two sets of officials in government positions, with Wolfley's finally winning out.

What's all this turmoil have to do with the Coconino County bill? The bill itself passed easily, having popular support behind it. However, Governor Wolfley vetoed it, declaring it unfair to Yavapai County. He believed the newly conceived Coconino County should take over more of Yavapai's debt. The people in Flagstaff were outraged to the point that they built a straw dummy and hung a sign reading "Governor Wolfley" on it. They hoisted the scarecrow up a pole near the train depot and then started a bonfire underneath. More than a few men commenced firing pistols into the air, creating a dramatic, riotous scene that lasted several hours. Passengers on the incoming train were so frightened that many stayed put, fearing a lynch mob. Wolfley didn't fare so well as governor either; he was forced to resign in August 1890 due to widespread unpopularity.

Flagstaff was not giving up on creating its new county. Encouraged by columns in the *Champion*, local leaders formed a committee to meet with officials from Prescott to discuss terms of splitting the land. The groups bargained hard, and it was finally agreed that Coconino County—if duly formed—would assume one-third of Yavapai's debt. A bill was drafted and presented to the Sixteenth Arizona Territorial Legislature, which began on January 19, 1891. Governor John Irwin had been appointed to replace Wolfley, and he signaled early support for the bill, which he signed on

February 19, 1891. While the town was ecstatic, other issues loomed large before the assembly and were taking their share of its attention. Arizona was coming closer to achieving statehood, though the 1891 bill died in the U.S. Senate. Arizona would try again, and that meant bringing the territory into compliance with federal standards. To that end, the assembly's opening address took aim at reducing costs of both the territorial prison and insane asylum. These areas were of growing concern because of funding and taxation. The seat of the newly formed Coconino County would soon face fallout from both issues.

The new county was huge, over 18,600 square miles, and included forests and grasslands and parts of the Grand Canyon. Flagstaff began building its courthouse, deciding on a majestic two-story red sandstone building, which served Coconino faithfully for over 125 years. An air of enthusiasm permeated the town with its designation as the county seat, and the people began enacting local ordinances and building infrastructure. Local historians cite the town meeting on May 21, 1894, as a benchmark in cementing Flagstaff's character and its direction forward. It was also when the town voted on building the reform school authorized (some say dictated!) by the Seventeenth Territorial Assembly.[26]

To be clear, a reform school was a penal institution, albeit for young people. The one proposed was specifically designated for teenage boys. Crime was on the minds of territorial constituents, and there was a racial element to the concern. A bounty for the capture of the notorious Apache Kid actually made it into an assembly bill that year. However, there were also bands of rustlers and robbers that attracted young Anglo males. When youths were captured, the courts separated them from the adults and attempted to rehabilitate the youngsters. The offenders were held in a juvenile detention center, or reform school, for however much time designated. Tribal boarding schools are a whole other topic—many were the Native American equivalent of a reform school. They remain a shameful mark against the Anglo culture, and the abuses suffered within reverberate through Native culture today. The reader can find well-resourced articles on these entities online.

Back to Act 81, "To Establish a Territorial Reform School for Juvenile Offenders and to provide Funds Therefor." The appointed territorial board chose railroad land situated about a half-mile south of downtown Flagstaff. At the 1894 meeting, $400 was raised to pay for the land. The reader may not be surprised to learn that while the money to proceed was raised within ten minutes, no one was thrilled with the idea of a reform school here. However, cooler minds convinced the town that it would be in Flagstaff's interest to have a large, beautiful building built at territorial expense. Two new educational facilities had been planned for Tucson and Tempe, and Flagstaff's town council had their eye on a similar prize.

Dealing with the peculiarities of the territorial assemblies was tricky, given their unstable nature. At the time, they were eminently preoccupied with Arizona's reach for statehood. Flagstaff was fortunate to have sophisticated representatives who deftly steered the assembly when it came to the town's interests. The Eighteenth Assembly created a Board of Territorial Control, which combined the oversight of the territorial prison, reform schools and insane asylums under its umbrella. All the while, in the northlands, the beautiful Moenkopi sandstone reform school sat empty and unfinished at the edge of town. It still needed windows and required a bit of interior work. The building was not slated to be completed any time soon though—town officials saw to that. Once the building was finished, the reform school would have to be opened. Then in 1896, the Nineteenth Territorial Assembly converted Flagstaff's still empty reform school into an insane asylum.

The town had been dragging its collective feet, loath to house Arizona's teenaged hoodlums inside the county. Locals entertained grander aspirations

NAU's Old Main as it sat, incomplete, awaiting its fate from the territorial assembly. *Courtesy NAU Archives, Cline Library. Item no. 1963; Call no. NAU.ARC. 1898.1..2.*

for the building as the town grew in size and popularity. Percival Lowell had built his observatory on Mars Hill, and what with the astronomers, geologists and biologists attracted to the Northlands, the council wanted to start a summer science school. However, even though they tried, they could not get a program in place before the Nineteenth Assembly convened.

Pluto Dome at Lowell Observatory. Dr. Lowell was wooed by the town to build his observatory atop of Mars Hill. *Library of Congress, Historic American Buildings Survey.*

There was already one asylum in Arizona, and the legislature envisioned Flagstaff as being a branch of the Phoenix location. Just as with the reform school, there was no appetite locally for housing the mentally ill in the red-brick building. The town quietly rebelled, and even the insane asylum board chimed in that there was a surplus of beds available in Phoenix. There was enough sentiment against it that one wonders if then Governor Franklin bore a grudge against Flag for some slight and wanted to impose a punishment.

Fortunately, the town didn't have to stew in an atmosphere of doubt and panic over the fate of the red-brick building. When the Twentieth Arizona Legislature convened in 1899, Governor Oakes Murphy presided over the body. Murphy was favorably disposed toward Flagstaff, having been skillfully wooed and impressed by various townspeople. The governor asked the assembly to designate the building for use as a normal school or sell it. House speaker Henry F. Ashurst introduced Bill 41 of reallocation: "To Establish the Northern Arizona Normal School and Provide for Its Maintenance." The bill was passed and signed into law on March 11, 1899, much to the glee of the locals. For decades after, the story of how the town outwitted and outwaited the territorial legislature was chuckled over. This iconic building, part of NAU's Old Main, still stands today, as proud and beautiful as it was in the 1890s.

5

THE LOCAL NEWSPAPER

Merriam Webster defines *wicked* as "morally, very bad." Evil. Fierce and / or vicious. Vile and unpleasant. Further definitions are more nuanced: going beyond reasonable or predictable limits, very fast. Finally, there's the playful use of the word as an adjective: disposed to or marked by mischief. Roguish. In northern Arizona, one place to find wickedness on full display was inside the local newspapers. From the late 1800s through the twentieth century, Flagstaff's been blessed with several periodicals that have made it a point to keep the town honest. They did this by calling out corruption, fingering individuals for bullying and criminal behavior, examining city spending, and so on. Most articles were well-written and concise, laying out information in an easily digestible manner. The pages were also filled with plenty of lighthearted material, and it's here you can find some pithy headlines. I've scoured the archives and found great examples of literary wickedness as defined by *Webster*. However, a short history of the Flagstaff newspapers will help ground the excerpts in their time and space.[27]

The *Coconino Sun*, a weekly paper that morphed into the *Arizona Daily Sun* in the 1940s, was the mainstay, but there have been others. The *Arizona Champion* was first published in Peach Springs in 1882 by Artemus E. Fay, a seasoned editor from back east. According to Platt Cline, the Atlantic and Pacific Railroad had convinced Fay that Peach Springs was destined to be the big city in northern Arizona. The esteemed editor arrived and took a few months to look around before deciding differently. He moved the newspaper to Flagstaff and published the first issue from here on February 2, 1884. Cline made a point of declaring Fay's paper as "excellent" and of "Republican leanings." Fay remained editor until September 1885, when J.W. Spafford took over the post. George Tinker became editor of the *Champion* in 1886, where he remained until May 1891. At that time, C.M. Funston took over, and the newspaper was renamed the *Coconino Weekly Sun*.

The town had another newspaper available at the time; the *Flagstaff Democrat* was started in 1889. The two papers, the *Sun* and the *Democrat*, merged and became the *Flagstaff Sun-Democrat*. After a few years, the

The *Coconino Weekly Sun*, October 3, 1895. *Library of Congress, Chronicling America.*

newspaper underwent another editorial change and was renamed the *Coconino Sun*. Several other papers circulated during the late 1890s and early 1900s—the town was nothing if not well-informed—but the *Sun* won out. While all its editors were important in their time, Fred S. Breen—who became editor and publisher in 1908—is often thought of as the first one who had staying power. He remained in his position until 1932, when both the *Sun* and the town were firmly established in northern Arizona. After he left, a series of editors filled the position as a new owner, Columbus Giragi, took over. Giragi sold the newspaper in 1946 to the W.G. McGiffin Company, and the entity morphed into the *Arizona Daily Sun*. Enter Platt Cline, beloved editor, reporter and later publisher of the *Sun*, who also authored Flagstaff's two most popular history books: *They Came to the Mountain* and *Mountain Town*. Cline passed in 2001 at age ninety, well after Northern Arizona University named its Cline Library in his honor.

The true history nerd will be disappointed that I've neglected several other northern Arizona newspapers. These are the topics that make up dissertations, so by necessity I've omitted the lesser-known ones. However, anyone interested can research the *Flag*, the *Frisco Signal* and the *Flagstaff Gem*. For now, let's dig into the *Coconino Weekly Sun*, the *Coconino Sun*'s predecessor, which was published on Thursdays from 1891 to 1896. These publications can be found online, along with issues of the *Arizona Champion*, in the Library of Congress archives.

It's a hoot to read through past issues of one of Flagstaff's earliest papers. The first two years the front page resembled an ad sheet, with Arizona Lumber & Timber occupying prime space. The Atlantic and Pacific Railroad and Levi Strauss were also mainstays but with smaller ads. The front-page format seldom varied those years, with publishing information on the left-hand side and, beneath in a vertical column, professional services offered by doctors, dentists and attorneys. Below those advertisers were the "Secret Societies," which consisted of five or six lodges or posts, whose meeting times and dates were signed by an officer.

I.O.O.F.—Flagstaff Lodge, No. 11, meets every Saturday evening in Odd Fellows' Hall. Visiting brethren cordially invited. A.H. Beasley, N.G. J.A. Vail, Secretary.

Also on the front page was a column titled "Territorial Notes." Included here were newsy blurbs from all of Arizona:

On Christmas day at Phoenix Dan O'Leary stabbed Stoney Harris, and the wounds may prove fatal.[28]

Wilcox has two stores conducted by Chinamen. They assume the ways of their successful colleagues by advertising.[29]

The Tucson jail contains 48 prisoners.[30]

H. Gill, a Los Angeles capitalist, has in contemplation the erection of a large brewery in Phoenix.[31]

Many of these early issues were focused on law and order, which was natural considering there was so little of it. Killings and murders were covered in depth, often with colorful hyperbole. Territorial meetings were keenly watched and reported on, with personal observations reserved for the page 3 "Current Comment" column. As noted in chapter 4, there was a lot at stake in those early years. Legislation coming out of the assemblies was a popular and sometimes hotly debated topic.

Within a few years, the format of the *Coconino Weekly Sun* changed slightly, but the number of ads displayed only grew. And what ads they were! The most entertaining were usually for remedies:

Mrs. Phoebe Johnson of Junction City, Ill., was told by her doctors she had consumption and that there was no hope for her, but two bottles of Dr. King's New Discovery completely cured her, and she says it saved her life. Mr. Thomas Eggers, 139 Florida street, San Francisco, suffered from a dreadful cold, approaching consumption, tried without result everything else, then brought one bottle of Dr. King's New Discovery and in two weeks was cured.

Walked with Crutches. Rheumatism—Eczema—Swelled Neck—Hood's Cured.
"For two years I have been sick, having been confined to the home for a year. I have had eczema for nine years, having skilled physicians, but received no benefit….Last July I commenced to use Hood's Sarsaparilla, and before I had finished one bottle, I laid the crutches aside. After taking two bottles the eczema had left me and I was almost entirely free from the effects of a swelled neck."

Knowledge brings comfort and improvement and tends to personal enjoyment when rightly used. The many who live better than others and enjoy life more, with less expenditures, by more promptly adapting the world's best products to the needs of the physical being will attest to the value to health of the pure liquid laxative principles embraced in the remedy, Syrup of Figs.[32]

All of these products, along with many more, were available at D.J. Brannen's drugstore. At first glance, some of the advertisements looked and read like news stories. Others, such as a piece extolling St. Jacobs Oil for rheumatism, were clearly formatted as a cheerful box ad. When the newspaper merged with the *Flagstaff Democrat* in late 1896, new owner Jerome Jones again changed the focus, and the ads took a back seat behind territorial reports. As the ownership teetered back and forth, so did the look of the paper. By 1908, the *Coconino Sun* seems to have struck a balance between all the departments that make up a respectable news operation. It had the look and gravitas to rival any other weekly paper.

What about ethnic prejudices? The *Sun* had its share, especially during its first two decades. Native Americans were frequently called "Injuns" or "savages," and many of the stories were centered on their violence or their demise. Hispanics fared better, although ugly adjectives such as "crazy" and "drunken" often preceded their identity. Again, the focus of those stories was demeaning and hardly newsworthy, seemingly printed more for entertainment than information. African Americans were similarly disrespected, and stories from back east centered on "Negro lynching" and crime. Sometimes negative opinions were couched in a piece of reporting. Here follows an item from the *Coconino Weekly Sun*:

The Indian is degenerating. Several years ago when an outbreak occurred it generally took a couple of thousand soldiers and a long period of time to quell it. The other day an uprising occurred in North Dakota which was suppressed in fifteen minutes by a posse of deputy marshals.

Sexual discrimination—and by that, I mean regarding women—was more nuanced. Whether this was a case of the paper reporting the news or the newspaper influencing the community is interesting. It's evident today, through historical remembrances such as Dr. Brannen's, the town wanted more "good" women to migrate to northern Arizona. The *Sun* appeared to cooperate by running family-friendly articles and depicting local women as hearty pioneers, à la Laura Ingalls. The paper's format around 1900 was complimentary to Flagstaff's female population, but their portrayal seems somewhat stereotypical. That tone began to change sometime in the mid-1920s.

Flagstaff had firmly developed an identity as a summer retreat and tourist destination by the '20s. This was reflected in every issue of the *Coconino Sun*, with articles frequently singing the town's praises. The focus on women's activities was now more diverse—softer yet more nuanced and stressing both the social and the professional. The personals were filled with reports on bridge parties, flower shows, afternoon teas and charitable events. Business leaders like Mary Costigan and professors such as Mary Boyer were quoted as authorities. They and other women were given news space by reporter Billie Yost, another Flagstaff trailblazer. This fleshed-

By June 1919, the *Sun* had evolved to include more local news. *Library of Congress, Chronicling America.*

out coverage of women's affairs continued into the 1930s and was quite different from the previous two decades. The 1930s were a strange blend of increased feminine leisure as well as upward mobility and education. Reading the ads and the personals, it's obvious the town took pride in its identity as a pioneer settlement. The women used washers and driers and went to the beauty salon, but the old ways were still the norm. In an era that didn't really value self-reflection, it might have been hard to navigate the changes that modernity brought.

By the mid-1940s, new columns had begun to appear in the *Sun*, including one by Ruth Millett titled "We the Women." The column ran for years, appearing two to three days a week, full of pithy advice for the fairer sex:

> *Underweight women are poor marital risks, because too-thin women are usually jittery women. So says Dr. James F. Bender, director of the National Institute for Human Relations. If that is true—and statistics show that women who are 15 or more pounds underweight have an excessively high divorce rate—then American women have been choosing the wrong type of woman to admire and emulate. The too-thin woman is the Queen Bee in feminine circles....She also sets the pace for activities of the other women. It's the woman who says that she has to be constantly on the go who prods her sisters into taking on more activities than they can handle.*[33]

> *A woman is well on her way to wisdom when she realizes—*
> *That no woman can be all things to any man.*
> *That a good disposition is more important than beauty in holding a man through the years.*
> *That a woman's clothing can't give her an air of distinction. She gives that to the clothes.*
> *That a woman never really wins an argument with a man, even when she seems to.*[34]

> *One woman I know made these resolutions for New Years. It seems to me a good many other women would benefit by adopting them.*
> *To spend more time with the people she really likes and less time on people who don't really matter to her.*
> *To learn how to turn down an invitation or refuse to take on new duties.*
> *To refuse to hurry.*
> *To be content with less than perfection in herself and in those she loves.*[35]

There are years of Ruth Millet's columns published throughout the 1940s. Personally, I find them fascinating. They range from eye-rolling and hopelessly dated to brilliant and humorous. While Millet focused on how to keep one's house in order and one's man happy, her writing also spoke to women about maintaining their own identity. Since she was a local, and her column was so popular, it's reasonable to believe she resonated with the average Flagstaff woman.

What's "wicked" about a weekly women's column? Nothing so obvious as to deserve that condemnation. But the writings may have carried undue weight. With a population of six thousand throughout the 1940s and no interstate roads, Flagstaff was a bit of a cocoon. The town wasn't isolated, but it was distant and took some time to get to. The *Coconino Sun* was a robust, well-written newspaper that often printed strong opinions. It seems that the *Sun* both reflected the community and informed it and carried a lot of influence. Women whose views differed from Millet's might have found themselves alone in their own neighborhood, and lonely. I became engrossed in and fascinated by the town's paper when writing my first book, *Flagstaff's Walkup Family Murders*. The power of the personals pages struck me as similar to the "likes" and "dislikes" of today's social media. In the case of the Walkups, it was who was not mentioned as much as who was that reflected the tragedy.

Speaking of the personals, they were a literal tracking device on the town's population. Through the years, the column changed names and sometimes took up several pages, but it remained the literal town crier:

John Verkamp left yesterday for Cincinnati.[36]

Miss Lula Davis returned Monday from a week's visit with friends in Albuquerque.[37]

A large number of cowboys from the Verde were in town the latter part of the week—some of them celebrated.[38]

J.F. Hawks who was seriously ill the early part of the week is able to be out in the street.[39]

And then the editor would slip in the occasional diss:

An overplus of tramps have infested this section lately and they have been altogether too impudent and bold. A stone pile and hard labor will fix these "gentlemen" of leisure.[40]

They are undertakers no more. Mortician is the new name, and rhymes perfectly with physician.

There are a number of idle young men in Flagstaff, whether from force of circumstances or from choice the Sun does not know. Every young man should find something to do. In spending his time in idleness he loses more than his time, as he gets into habits that are hard to shake off.

By the 1930s, the "Local Brevities" and "Local and Personal" columns were mostly gossipy, while the Editor's Page contained the moral snipes and snarks.

I've culled a few of the funnier and more eclectic stories from Flagstaff's past, as written in the *Sun*:

If you have an old Waterbury watch which has kept you late for your meals since last October, take it out in the dark of the moon, on March 30th, hold it under the hydrant until it holds ups its hands and [sic] hour later. This is the daylight savings law, which is in direct contravention to the "moonshine" extravagance law.[41]

Tourism was now a major force in the region and often a focus of the newspaper. *Library of Congress, Chronicling America.*

Isabel Jemenez of Flagstaff sashayed into County Clerk Tom L. Rees' office last Friday, with a pretty girl on his arm, and got a marriage license. Then someone wised him up that the license would be a dangerous thing to monkey with until he could show along with it a decree of divorce from his present wife. So Isabel deferred his hopes a while and got Frank Gold busy next day filing a suit for divorce. He says he was married in old Mexico in 1904 and his wife left him, that he doesn't know where she went, or where she is, or anything else about her.[42]

"99 3/4% Americans Not Worth a Damn and They Know It." This statement made by Lieut. J.A. Crozier during his lecture last Friday night met with hearty approval from the large audience in attendance. Lieut. Crozier spent several months on the front line…from personal observations painted an awful picture of the cruelties practiced by the Huns. He stated that every person in this country must come to realize the big job ahead of the Allies…and do their part, either at home or in France.[43]

"Beating Way to Mother for Christmas Former Wealthy Stockman Meets Accidental Death Here"
Beating his way hurriedly two-thirds across the continent to eat his Christmas dinner with his little old invalid mother in California, Wm. N. Hobson, until after the war one of the wealthiest stockmen in Missouri, was so severely injured in Flagstaff Friday night trying to jump fast mail train No. 7 that he died within an hour. From one of the sections of No. 7 Hobson alighted on the far side of the depot. He kept out of sight of the crowd but made some inquiries about the speed of the various trains. Then, as another section of the No. 7 was pulling out, he tried to get onboard. The train must have been going faster than he thought; or perhaps he was numb with cold; or he may have stumbled and found himself unable to regain his footing. He was dragged a hundred feet or so.[44]

"Find Incipient Brandy Under Floor"
When Fred V. Plomteaux, of Cliffs, gets back from Santa Fe, where he went a few days ago on vacation, he will find that the sanctity of his domicile has been badly tampered with and its parfum de fascination removed. Because (the authorities) went out to Cliffs on Wednesday and called on Plomteaux in his absence. A neat little trap door led into a hole underneath the floor. Here was a bottle of Peach mash, with a couple of lanterns and a lot of horse manure to keep it warm, sizzly and properly stinky.[45]

"Holds Mirror to Insure Good Aim in Shooting Self; Sister Lives Here"
With a steel mirror to make sure that his aim was good, and a .32
automatic Colts revolver, Adolphus R. King, formerly a wealthy ranchman
and stockman of Edgar, Colo., committed suicide near Coons Tank.[46]

Below are several headliners from the same paper, the *Coconino Sun*, January 4, 1924:

"Gabaldon Wanted to Kill Himself but His Aim Was Bum; Has a Sore Head; Maybe Was Love Affair"

"Harry Wade Improving and Dink Smith Who Shot Him also Mending"

"If She Hadn't Changed Her Clothes Would Have Got Away; Did Anyway"

Fred Breen's paper definitely had a cheeky air about it. However, it also included countless items that may have seemed trivial but are informative when read today.

"Grave of Lewis Aikin, Noted Artist, Faces North Toward His Beloved Frisco Peaks"
The grave of Lewis Aikin lies north and south in the Flagstaff cemetery while all other graves lie east and west. For before he died Mr. Akin asked that he might be buried facing the San Francisco peaks which had been his great inspiration in life.[47]

In 1925, Breen undertook an ambitious world travel agenda. He then sent letters that were published in the *Sun* in a front-page column titled: "Col. F. S. Breen's [fill in the installment number] Around-the-World Letter." In each he detailed his voyages, the people he met, their customs and the terrain of the land, be it Turkey, China, Hong Kong, Japan, India or elsewhere. Breen was an entertaining writer with an astute eye for details, and these letters ran for months. Even their titles were intelligent and humorous:

"Shrines and Temples Thick as Freckles on a Kid"[48]

"Women Are Very Convenient in Japan, Children Plentiful and Handkerchiefs Absent"[49]

Coconino Sun, April 3, 1925. The front page features one of Colonel Breen's "travelogues." *Library of Congress, Chronicling America.*

"China Has Many Idols, Also Much Wretchedness and Suffering"[50]

"Rolling Marbles with Chinese Kids; then Across Earth's Belly-band where King Neptune Holds Court"[51]

If the reader is interested in following Fred Breen's fascinating travelogue, you can find archives of the *Sun* in the Library of Congress's Chronicling America collection. These are available online, and the material would take a lifetime to consume.

It's apparent that as the *Sun* matured and evolved into the *Arizona Daily Sun*, the articles—while still informative—became much drier. It could be that as Flagstaff found its footing there was much less wild in the New West. The *Sun* remained the primary source of local news and government well into the early 2000s. Then the rise of social media began and various platforms knocked the paper about, almost toppling it. Even while I was researching and writing *Wicked Flagstaff*, the *Daily Sun* underwent two major changes, which locals view as upheavals in their ordered lives. Editor Chris Etling had the thankless task of paring down the frequency of the paper's print version to three days a week. Later, he was at the helm in 2023 when the paper was sold to Wick Communications. There's been a lot of grumbling; old habits die hard. And for many of us, there's no more pleasant and entrenched habit than reading the local paper over a cup of coffee. So far it seems that Flagstaffians, as suspicious and cranky as ever, have given grudging support to the new face on our old friend. I guess we'll see.

TUNNELS BENEATH THE TOWN

$\mathcal{W}$hy are we humans intrigued by going underground and searching out the hidden and forbidden? I don't know, but we field countless questions from our guests on Freaky Foot Tours about the infamous Flagstaff tunnels. Many stories are passed around about when they were built, how they were used and whether any remain open today. What's not readily available is factual information on any or all of the above. The tunnels have taken on a life of their own, and I'm often surprised by what I hear about their history. So this chapter takes a deep dive into the dark passages below Flagstaff in an attempt to flush out some answers.[52]

To begin with, yes—there is a tunnel system beneath historic downtown. These tunnels are mainly used to run utilities, such as gas, electrical and water lines. There are also tunnels that served as a passageway between some of the earlier buildings and storefronts. Almost all of these are either blocked off or filled in, with a rumored one or two exceptions. There's a YouTube video, "The Forgotten Underground," by Arizona filmmaker Nikki Charnstrom, that's a must-see for any tunnel enthusiast. From my own research and findings, Charnstrom seems to have captured the actual story of Flag's unseen mystery that many want to romanticize.

Like most towns, Flagstaff was built in stages. Old Town was erected during pre-railroad years, in anticipation of the men and money that would come into the area as the rails were laid. At that time, all buildings (such that they were) sat aboveground—no need for any tunnels here. When railroad officials decided to make Flagstaff a water stop, they set up a boxcar station to the east of Old Town, where the ground was flatter. Entrepreneurs were quick to grasp that this was the location to build their stores. It was around 1883 that businesses began to appear across the street from the station, along today's Route 66. This shift from Old Town's tent city to the permanent buildings in what was then prime real estate ushered in the need for infrastructure.

This is a good place to slip in a short history of the three great fires of the 1880s. These infernos affected the new settlement and its people, decimating much of Old Town and the buildings along Front Street. The fires also stirred up prejudices against the Chinese people who'd settled here.[53] This history likely started one tunnel rumor that is alive to this day, that these underground passageways were escape tunnels for the Chinese.[54]

The first fire was on July 22, 1884, and it almost destroyed Old Town. The wooden structures fell like flaming dominos, one after the other, as the wind whipped the blaze into an inferno. The fire was blamed on a "female in a dance hall" who carelessly knocked over a lamp. By then, New Town (today's historic downtown) was firmly established as the business district, although homes were beginning to appear here too. Alarmed by the destruction, New Town hired a nightwatchman to alert the people to signs of smoke as they slept. However, after six months, the post was quietly vacated. The second disaster occurred on February 14, 1886, and this time it was New Town that went up in flames. According to headlines, thirty buildings were destroyed in thirty minutes. Even worse, a popular young man, William Bidinger, burned to death in the back of Berry's saloon.

This was when the ugly prejudices against the Chinese surfaced with a vengeance. It's a sad fact that the Chinese people faced ill will throughout the West. Flagstaff was no different than other settlements, although no excessive hostility had been reported up to this point. After the February fire, an article in the *Champion* stated that the flames were first seen on the roof of the Chinese restaurant that was in Berry's building. When the owner, Sam Kee, was questioned, he said he and his assistants had fled the building when they discovered the fire. The paper itself fanned the public's anger by suggesting the men should have raised the alarm immediately. It also implied that not doing so had caused more extensive damage and possibly cost Bidinger his life. Finally, there was a suggestion that the Chinese might have started the fire on purpose. These accusations seeped into the town's consciousness, and anger began to build. Soon a call for all Chinese to leave town within twenty-four hours was issued to Hop Sing, the acknowledged leader of their group.

Right: Tourists seem to be enthralled with the tunnel system downtown, and this sidewalk outside Babbitt's store offers a peek below. *Author's collection.*

Below: There was a bowling alley in the basement of the Masonic building as well as a tunnel. It's said the tunnel has been filled in. *Author's collection.*

Most of the Chinese people gathered their belongings and took the train west to Williams. However, a few of the elders stayed in town, ostensibly to settle debts and sell property. The lumber mill asked for and was given leeway, as they employed a number of Asian domestics who couldn't be quickly replaced. According to the *Champion*, this began a kind of back-and-forth movement of the Chinese people, who slowly returned to town only to be "told" to leave again. The pattern repeated itself, with periods of intensity, over the next two years until sentiment cooled. The Chinese had an advocate in Emma Gonzales, who wrote letters to the editor denouncing the bashing:

> *In answer to the above anonymous letter received this A.M. (in which the lady was commanded to get the Chinamen out of her house within ten days or else) written by a person or persons styling themselves "Committee" on the Chinese question, I have only this to say. That if another spasmodic eviction of Chinese is to convulse Flagstaff, let it be so, but don't think for a moment to bulldoze me by such letters, much less to make me your servant. Every man, woman or child our government welcomes to our ports, so far as I am concerned, shall know the meaning of* Three Cheers for the Red, White and Blue.[55]

Gonzales proved to be a thorn in the side of Flagstaff officials many a time and on various issues. She spoke for at least a few others regarding treatment of the Chinese and was known for sticking up for the underdog against the prevailing establishment.

There was one final "great" fire in July 1888 and several smaller, albeit destructive, ones in 1889. Per the newspaper and other historic accounts, if there was grumbling against the Chinese regarding these it was kept to a mutter. The point about the fires and prejudicial treatment of the Chinese people is that, yes, it existed. However, despite popular opinion today linking them to the tunnel system as an escape route or hideout, there's no evidence of that. The Chinese were blamed and run out of town after the 1886 inferno, but many returned. None of the families set up housing in the tunnels below. All in all, it is a sad piece of Flagstaff's past. As historian Joe Meehan said,

> *They had restaurants and laundries; their Chinese cemetery was in the area now occupied by the Adult Center. Every time that there was a fire, you blamed the outsiders. The Chinese had laundries and restaurants that used*

wood fires. But it seems they (the town) failed to realize that everyone did. Everyone cooked and heated with wood burning stoves.

As I wrote at the beginning of this chapter, there are—or were—a few tunnels constructed for nefarious purposes in downtown. The Corner Tavern, formerly Majerle's Sports Bar, sits at the crossroads of Route 66 and North San Francisco Street. The building was constructed in 1883 and, going by the Sanborn Fire Insurance maps, has served as a saloon, drugstore, pool hall and restaurant. It has a basement office where, sealed behind a nondescript wall, the entry to an authentic "escape tunnel" exists. It was used by gamblers when the law caught wind that an illicit poker party was underway. If the sheriff came to the front desk wanting a look downstairs, the manager triggered a device that alerted the players in the basement. The gamblers could escape through the secret door and were often successful at eluding capture. The tunnel was about a half-block long and ran north, coming up from the floor inside another building. This tunnel has been sealed for some time, at least at the Corner Tavern's end. It features prominently in the YouTube video "The Forgotten Underground."[56]

Another passageway that was used for scandalous purposes is under South San Francisco Street. The building at 28 East Benton Avenue is the historic Paso Del Norte, former brothel turned office complex. Dan Duke's body piercing and tattoo shop is located inside on the northwest corner, and an employee there in 2018 told me several intriguing stories. A tunnel, which was only partially sealed, runs from the Paso Del Norte's basement under San Francisco Street to the building across the way. Apparently, that establishment was once a male boardinghouse although today it serves as a community mission. The tunnel was a surreptitious passageway for men and women to travel unseen and meet to indulge in some guilty pleasures. The eager storyteller led me down several crumbling steps to a basement area, where I did see what appeared to be a half-filled tunnel entry. This was an illicit adventure and sadly we were redirected upstairs before I could take a look around. I've never been invited back to explore and—frankly—wouldn't stake a bet on what that opening actually was. However, given the history of the area south of the tracks, it probably is a relic from the red-light district.

There are a few other documented tunnels in town, albeit ones that were considered legitimate passageways. The Babbitt Brothers had at least one short tunnel at North San Francisco and Birch Avenue that served as a connector between two of their businesses. Flagstaff winters can be snowy, cold and windy—not to mention the ice that accrues on the sidewalks. According to local historians, several of the downtown merchants utilized tunnels for travel between buildings in foul weather. Almost all of these passageways have been filled in or blocked off. I was kindly shown the one in the basement of the Weatherford Hotel a few years ago when researching *Haunted Flagstaff*. This passageway is on the west wall of the Gopher Hole and leads approximately seventy-five feet to an opening in the Orpheum Theatre. John Weatherford built the underpass for the comfort of his hotel guests who might have wanted to take in an evening show during the winter. Today, the mouth of the tunnel is concealed behind a door and filled with giant boulders, at least on the hotel's side.

The remains of a passageway beneath South San Francisco Street connecting today's Mission (*left*) and Paseo del Norte (*right*) cannot be accessed. *Author's collection.*

John Weatherford built an underground tunnel from the basement of the Weatherford Hotel to his Orpheum Theatre. *Author's collection.*

Then there are the utility tunnels that are accessed by city workers and others for inspection and repair. These passageways are large enough in areas for a grown man to stand up, as evident from the aforementioned YouTube video. There have been credible reports of opium pipes, gambling devices and clothing being discovered within; however, are the dice and pipes from the 1910s or the 1970s? A former city employee who inspected the tunnels around 2007 told me that it's easy to imagine teenagers from the '60s and '70s gaining access and holding a secret rendezvous below. This engineer admitted that drug and gambling paraphernalia were found scattered about. He said, though, that there was nothing to suggest these were leftover remnants of Chinese opium dens. As for the tunnels being used as hidden living quarters for unfortunate refugees, my friend just laughed. "That's a big no-way," he said.

Another piece of history adds to the legends of Flagstaff's underground maze and offers a timeline. In 1920, the Flagstaff Electric Company began the process of laying steam mains to the businesses and hotels in order to provide them with steam heating. Up to this point, most had used wood-burning stoves and fireplaces, which were dangerous and inefficient. Owned by the Riordans, who also owned Arizona Lumber & Timber, the electric company proposed burning leftover sawdust to provide heating to the downtown merchants. This system reduced the risk of wood fires and coincidentally gave Chinese residents some protection against accusations involving rogue stove fires. The new system also supplied heat to the burgeoning Teacher's College just south of the tracks. NAU still has a system of tunnels and underground passageways, but that's a whole other story for another time. In any event, 1920 was well after Flagstaff's frightening period of catastrophic fires, thus debunking again the myth that the Chinese used these as escape passages.

The buildings along Railroad Avenue had many tunnels, some used for utilities and others as passageways. *Library of Congress online catalog; photographer Jack Delano.*

After digging about and researching the always popular, ever-intriguing subject of the town's tunnels, I've come to the same conclusion that I started with. Utility tunnels exist and are in use today, but they were built decades after the fires so were not used as escape routes by the Chinese. Were they used in later years for illicit activities by locals who had access? It seems so. Then there are the legitimate passageways built by various businesses downtown, almost all of which have been blocked off. Underground tunnels were also built for nefarious purposes, usually involving gambling and prostitution, and it appears they too have been sealed.

I've been told by various locals that they worked at such-and-such place in Flag and that they know there are tunnels beneath the stores. I've found information that might reconcile their memories with what I found through research. Historic downtown has many old buildings that have basements. Several of these buildings that once had connecting passageways also had/have a basement storeroom. Some of these rooms are recessed far enough into the foundation that they may have been mistakenly thought to be a tunnel. This is how I'm going to leave it, as so much of the infrastructure is inaccessible now. Opinions regarding the tunnels are deeply held, and we tend to believe what makes the most sense to us. In the end, the mystery and romance that surrounds them calls to our imagination and makes the past a little more alive.

THE UNSOLVED MURDER OF DUTCH MAY

Much like Commodore Perry Owens, Dutch May Peters Prescott was a real character. She was also an anomaly in 1900s Flagstaff and a woman who—if not ahead of her time—made the best of them. Dutch was definitely a madam, possibly a prostitute, and actually owned a number of properties south of the tracks. Information on her is hard to come by, but the circumstances of her death made front-page news.[57]

It was a lovely summer's afternoon, August 30, 1916. Dutch May had wanted to build a new home and decided on a lot just north of the shack house she presently occupied. Dutch had recently married her longtime companion, a Mr. Prescott, or at least this was the story going round. The couple's friends said the two were vague about when the blessed event occurred and had, in fact, been squabbling quite a bit lately. Apparently, Prescott had a way with the ladies and a touch of wanderlust, traits his new wife didn't appreciate. In any event, Dutch had employed local man Everett Hanna to draw up the plans for the new home she and Prescott wanted to build. That afternoon, Hanna was on his way to clarify a few of the specs with the madam. As he approached the front entry of the shack, Hanna caught a whiff of something peculiar. He knocked at Dutch's door several times and, when no one answered, became alarmed enough to go fetch Judge Harrington. Harrington was the town coroner, and after hearing Hanna's story, he hurried over to Dutch's house, just south of the tracks.

This is close to the area (if not exactly) of Dutch May's shack, where she and Prescott were found murdered. *Author's collection.*

When Harrington arrived, he too detected a foul odor coming from inside, mingled with the smell of burnt cloth. He wasted no time in breaking down the front door. Upon entering the couple's modest abode, Harrington was met with a horrific sight. Blood was splattered from floor to ceiling in the small room, with a bloody razor found on the floor. Dutch May's beloved dog lay dead, killed by a bullet, and her pet canary lay lifeless in its cage. As he moved toward the bedroom, Judge Harrington discovered an even more gruesome scene.

The lifeless couple were lying on their bed, Dutch huddled against Prescott as if seeking protection. He was holding a six-shooter in his hand, fully loaded except for the cartridge under the hammer. Both bodies were badly burned and charred from a fire started on their bedclothes. That was not the cause of either one's death though. Dutch was shot twice through the head, and her throat was cut deep enough to have killed her outright. Prescott was shot at least once in the head and his throat cut from ear to ear. Other cuts and wounds were found on both bodies, giving the appearance of a fight. The room was drenched in blood, and a blood-soaked note was found on a dresser. Printed in the September 1 *Sun*, it read:

> *May and I quarreled over a P.I. that always came here and tried to break up our home, and she attacked me with a razor which is around here somewhere. I shot her then myself. Notify Mrs. P.L. Prescott 325 Garfield Ave. K.C. Mrs. C.M. Prescott, Santa Barbara, Cal.*

No one in town believed the contents of the note, if for no other reason than that feat would have been impossible. Prescott would have had to kill Dutch and then shoot himself after deeply cutting his own throat (or vice versa). Then he'd have to start a fire in the room, climb into the bed, reload the gun and light both himself and Dutch on fire with a match. Yet the writing appeared to be Prescott's. (By the way, that's the only name we have for Dutch's companion.) Not only that, but the *Sun* also noted that the handwriting appeared to be unhurried, as "the letters were formed smoothly and on even lines with capital letters and general makeup of letters found addressed to his wife in her trunk."

In the immediate aftermath of the murders, there was a thorough investigation, which was reported on in the *Sun*. Dutch May was a madam who was liked by many and tolerated by most in Flagstaff. She owned several brothels and was known as being good to her girls and keeping the riffraff at bay. The town was shocked by the cruel, heartless murder of the couple. Again, from the September 1 *Coconino Sun*:

> *"Dutch May" Peters, as she was known here before being married to Prescott some months ago, has lived here a good many years and had accumulated considerable property in the restricted district. She had the reputation of being peacefully inclined, with no enemies.*

By the following week's newspaper, Prescott had been demoted in print to Dutch's "supposed husband" after more information was gathered by the coroner's jury. It seems that the Mrs. C.M. Prescott of Santa Barbara was actually Prescott's wife and there was a child as well. Yet even with this grave deception and reports of the couple fighting before the incident, the murder-suicide scenario seemed improbable.

A clue was found inside a corrugated iron storehouse located behind the murder shack. There was blood splattered on the floor and walls and a bloody handprint on the door, which was found standing open that

Dutch May owned several brothels south of the tracks, including two buildings original to this corner at 19 South San Francisco Street. *Author's collection.*

afternoon. Nothing else was disturbed inside the storeroom, a fact that puzzled the jury. Another strange bit of evidence was Dutch May's trunk, which contained her clothing and jewelry. It was found open and had been rifled through, again by someone with bloody hands. Not only were expensive pieces of jewelry left in the trunk, but a bloody gun was found inside as well. All these anomalies, along with the fire, the multiple wounds, the note and the killing of Dutch's pets, led to the jury's conclusion "that the deceased came to their deaths by knife and gunshot wounds inflicted by parties unknown."

That was the official report. Rumors began to circulate almost immediately, and it was whispered that a "Flagstaff official" may have been involved in the pair's murders. The *Sun* alluded to the same once and then the story was quashed. Much like the Walkup murders, which occurred some twenty years later, the aftermath of the tragedy was buried along with the victims. In the case of Dutch May Peters Prescott and her companion, their murders remained unsolved and unavenged. Dutch's father wrote that he could not afford to send for her remains and asked that the town bury her. As for Mr. Prescott, no family members came

A closer look at what is now the Downtowner Hotel and Grand Canyon Hostel. The shack where the murder took place is to the north. *Author's collection*.

forward to claim his body. Both of the victims are buried in Potters Field at Citizens Cemetery.

After her death, at least one of Dutch's brothels was brought by K.J. Nackard. Nackard owned hotels and commercial property and the former house of ill-repute was renovated into a building that would be used as part of his hotel complex, the Nackard Auto Inn. The exact location where Dutch and Mr. Prescott met their demise is confusing, as there were two brothels sharing the same address, 19 South San Francisco. Today the address is part of both the Grand Canyon Hostel and the Downtowner Hotel. I first heard this sad story on a 2015 self-guided tour of the south side. The gentleman who was stationed at Dutch's stop, Joseph Jordan, said the actual brothel was likely on a square of rocky dirt, close to the tracks. There have been reports of blinking lights and the smell of smoke coming from here, and the area has a reputation of being haunted. It's a stop on local ghost tours where guests hear the sad story of Dutch May and Mr. Prescott in Flagstaff's historic red-light district.[58]

THE TWA MEMORIAL

On June 30, 1956, a TWA Super-Constellation collided with a United Airlines DC-7 over the Grand Canyon National Park. The few remains recovered were helicoptered to Flagstaff to be tagged, catalogued and studied. The 128 people who died that balmy summer's day had no reason to suspect their lives were in danger. This was the golden age of air travel, when Americans were bombarded with ads glorifying the pleasures and safety of flying. However, behind all of the glamour and excitement the new frontier was generating lurked an element of carelessness. The airline industry had been growing rapidly, and there was increased danger in the unregulated skies. In the preceding years there had been several commercial airline disasters, including one collision on June 28, 1952. Many of these accidents resulted in the deaths of some or all of the passengers, yet the incidents were not well-publicized. While the government had been actively expanding its regulatory hand within aviation, it took the horrific event over the Grand Canyon to kick an underfunded system into high gear. This is the tragic story of an aviation accident and the effect it had on the families, a town and an industry.[59]

That Saturday morning was a cloudy one at Los Angeles International Airport (LAX). Captain Jack Gandy, a forty-one-year-old former navy pilot, arrived at the airport in anticipation of his flight from Los Angeles to Kansas City, Missouri. This was a routine run for Captain Gandy, who lived in Kansas City with his wife and four children. He would be flying TWA Flight 2's *Star of the Seine*, a Lockheed L-1049 Super Constellation, which

The majestic Grand Canyon, as seen from the south rim. The collision occurred in the skies in the upper-righthand corner of this image. *Author's collection.*

was known for its iconic triple tail, made up of three vertical stabilizers. At the airport, Gandy met with his flight crew at the TWA Dispatch Office. Besides the pilot, there was the first officer, James Ritner, thirty-one; flight engineer Forrest Breyfogle, thirty-seven; and flight attendants Beth Davis and Tracine Armbruster on the morning's run. Per usual, the flight plan, fuel requirements and alternative airports were reviewed, as well as the weather and any other pertinent information. They would carry sixty-five passengers that day, for a total of seventy on board.

Piloting United 718, the *Mainliner Vancouver*, was Captain Robert Shirley, forty-eight. The DC-7 Douglas aircraft was flying a routine route as well, with its first leg being LAX to Chicago's Midway. Captain Shirley arrived at the airport to meet with his crew in United's Dispatch Office, where the team scrutinized their flight plan. Shirley would be flying with first officer Robert Harms, thirty-six; flight engineer Girardo Fiore, thirty-nine; and flight attendants Margaret Shoudt and Nancy Kemnitz. As fate would have it, Harms was scheduled to work an earlier flight that day, but his assignment was switched to comply with a cap on monthly flying hours. As with the TWA officers, all three of the United cockpit crew were family men. When it took off, Flight 718 was carrying a total of fifty-eight souls.

There were slight delays to both of these routine flights that Saturday. The TWA Super-Connie, scheduled to depart at 8:30 a.m., needed a minor repair, which cost it thirty-one minutes. United 748, which was scheduled to take off at 8:45 a.m., actually departed at 9:04 a.m. The passengers boarded their respective planes as one did in 1956—that is to say, very differently than how we board today. There was no TSA in the 1950s—no scanners to walk through, no luggage checks. Neither was there a jet bridge that connected the gate to one's plane. When the flight was called over the airport's public announcement system, passengers lined up and exited the terminal (usually through a back door) and walked outside. They would continue walking alongside a fenced path to a portable stairway that was placed against the airplane, with steps leading up to its entryway. A flight attendant stood at the top step, greeting passengers with a smile, checking tickets and perhaps helping with luggage. This was, after all, the golden age of flying!

This is a good place to insert a brief history of air travel in the United States. The first commercial flight took place on January 1, 1914, on the St. Petersburg–Tampa Airboat Line. That first Airboat was an open-air, mostly wooden seaplane that was loud and uncomfortable at best. The flight lasted approximately twenty-four minutes and, in today's money, cost about $12,000. Needless to say, the price was prohibitive for most folks. Governments found a use for airplanes in World War I, which led to further developments, including the use of the two-way radio. After the war, many of the smaller planes were repurposed to transport mail. This was a lucrative business in the States, and once again, the feasibility of passenger transport entered the conversation. In 1926, concerns over safety led to Congress passing the Air Commerce Act. This allowed federal oversight and established regulations regarding pilot licensing, aircraft maintenance and some control over air space. However, it was really during World War II and in its aftermath that the industry grew by leaps and bounds. Radar had become an important tool for pilots and ground controllers, and now its use extended into commercial air travel. New materials for building aircrafts, cabin pressurization and bigger engines were available to private companies and evolving at a rapid pace. The industry was poised to take a leap into this exciting new era of air travel. While carrying mail and flying freight still paid the bills, passenger transport was now seen as the future.

Back to the tragic encounter between TWA Flight-2 and United 718 in June 1956. Despite the delays at LAX, both planes were soon airborne.[60] TWA lifted off three minutes before the United flight and headed east via Daggett, California, putting it on a slightly northeast trajectory. Meanwhile, United 718 headed toward Palm Springs on a directly eastward route. Crucial to this tragedy is that in 1956, controlled air space around LAX ended roughly 150 miles outside of the airport. Both flights were soon out of direct and centralized ATC radio contact, which gave the pilots a good deal of freedom in uncontrolled airspace. In the primitive system of that era, pilots outside of major airline hubs (Chicago, Los Angeles, Kansas City, etc.) and outside of controlled air space, communicated requests or information to their individual airline's flight dispatch center. That center would then contact regional ATC, who would answer the dispatch center, who would then contact the pilot with the information requested. This system was like a bad game of telephone with indirect communication that could be chaotic and was occasionally disastrous.

With both flights heading east and only minutes apart, several notable events occurred. TWA radioed its dispatch office at 9:21 a.m., asking to climb to twenty-one thousand feet. After the phone relay described above, the controllers denied the request, knowing that United was flying at that same altitude. However, before Captain Gandy received their reply, he radioed his dispatch office again, asking if he could fly "1,000 on top." This meant he was asking to fly one thousand feet above any cloud cover that was present and that he'd be using Visual Flight Rules (VFR). This request was okayed, putting the onus on TWA to see and avoid other aircraft. The controllers also advised Gandy that United 718 was in the area and flying at twenty-one thousand feet. Gandy radioed back an acknowledgement.[61]

Both flights were headed for the Painted Desert Line, the 173-mile-long invisible radii that ran between Arizona and Utah that was used by ATC as a reference point. It later appeared that ATC knew both planes were flying at roughly twenty-one thousand feet and would likely cross the line at the same time; however, they could pass over it anywhere along those 173 miles. What was not and could not be known were the choices the pilots would make when flying over the Grand Canyon.

As said before, these were the early days of commercial air travel. Both the airlines and the pilots wanted to provide exceptional service to their paying customers. While fine dining and plump pillows were part of the sell, so was a stunning bird's-eye view of the landscape below. And there aren't many more magnificent wonders than the Grand Canyon, stretching

277 miles across northern Arizona. Both TWA Flight 2 and United 718 would fly across a portion of the canyon on their respective routes, and it's understandable that Gandy and Shirley wanted to give their passengers a peek at this spectacular sight.

The collision occurred at approximately 10:30 a.m. A garbled transmission was picked up by United radio operators in Salt Lake City and San Francisco that sounded like, "Salt Lake, (ah), 718…we are going in!" In the background, a voice tentatively identified as Captain Shirley's was begging, "Pull up, pull up." Investigations into the crash pointed to towering cumulus clouds over the canyon around the time of the collision. This dense white air mass likely hid each plane from the other's sight until it was too late to react. The recovered wreckage gave investigators some evidence into the probable scenario that morning. It was speculated that both pilots had angled their respective crafts into a position where their passengers had a good view of the wonder below. Coming in at a twenty-five-degree angle (relative to each other) United 718 likely saw the TWA plane seconds before impact. Desperate to avoid the inevitable, Captain Shirley banked his plane hard to the right and pitched downward. TWA Flight 2 probably had no idea it was hit until the United's wing sheared off the Super-Connie's tail. Flight 2 made a nosedive into the canyon at an estimated seven hundred feet per second, slamming into a ravine near Temple Butte. The plane disintegrated on impact, leaving a debris field of twisted metal. The United DC-7's left wing had been mortally wounded, and the crippled airplane descended rapidly in a left spiral. It crashed into the south cliff of Chuar Butte, roughly a mile away from the Connie, killing all on board. Milford Hunter's iconic rendition of the two planes colliding in midair can be easily found on the internet and provides a detailed visual of the tragedy.

When neither pilot answered calls from dispatch, a general alert went out to other aircraft in the area. Palin Hudgin was flying over the canyon that morning, charging tourists fifteen dollars for a look at the Colorado River. He and his brother Henry operated Grand Canyon Airlines, a small air taxi service with a big name. He later testified that at about 12:15 p.m., he saw light smoke down inside the canyon. Hudgin thought little about it at the time and headed home for dinner. Later, when he heard over the radio that two planes had gone missing, he and Henry flew back to where he had seen the smoke. There was no mistaking the Super-Connie's triple tail, which lay on the canyon floor and was essentially intact. The brothers notified authorities, and by the following morning, the Grand Canyon was abuzz with helicopters, rescue workers and investigators from the Civil Aeronautics

The remains of the TWA tail sit on the canyon floor, separated from the main debris field by about five hundred yards. *Photo by unknown FAA investigator, 1956; commons.wikimedia.org*

Board. When the first officials reached the iconic TWA Constellation tail empennage, they noticed the tip of United's left wing sitting close by.

None of the 128 bodies were found intact, although a few of the remains were able to be identified. The most difficult crash site was United 718; scraps of the fuselage sat high on an edge of Chuar Butte, a notoriously rugged, remote area. The airlines hired a team of Swiss mountain climbers and the Swiss Air Rescue to access the site and bring down passenger remains and personal effects. Approximately 1.2 miles west lay the wreckage of the Constellation, its debris field several hundred yards away from the tail piece. Any human remains were gathered and put into rubber bags. Within forty-eight hours, a shuttle began between the canyon and Flagstaff, bringing the bags to a makeshift morgue for further processing.

The town was scrambling to accommodate the fallout from this unprecedented disaster. The collision was the largest loss of life to date in commercial air travel, and dealing with human remains and family members was the top priority. The National Guard was called to duty at the Coconino County Fairgrounds, where, under the supervision of the FBI, bits of bone, body parts and possessions were painstakingly examined by government and civil authorities as they came in. The sound of helicopters chopping southward from the Canyon was the norm that week. Locals who lived through those days said it was the saddest, loudest and most jumbled July the town had ever experienced. As bereaved family members arrived, they were joined by airline officials and the national press. And if all that wasn't overwhelming enough, July 2 was the official opening of Flagstaff's biggest summer event: the Southwest All-Indian Pow Wow.

I wrote about Pow Wow in my first book for The History Press, *Flagstaff's Walkup Family Murders*. In 1956, this annual summer event was in its twenty-seventh year and, as usual, had been eagerly anticipated. Pow Wow was an extravaganza of Native American rodeo, dancing, music and crafts and was hugely popular with people throughout the region. Hotels and campgrounds

The image of wagons carrying Native Americans to the annual Pow Wow is juxtaposed beneath the tragic headlines from the Canyon. *Courtesy of* Arizona Daily Sun.

had been sold out months prior to the event, which was traditionally held over Fourth of July weekend. There was not a bed to be found in or around Flagstaff when disaster struck in the canyon.

The call went out, at first through the *Daily Sun* and the chamber of commerce, then churches, neighborhoods and social groups. Locals were asked to open their doors to either victims' family members or Pow Wow attendees who found themselves without a room. Hotels and motels were asked, if at all possible, to double up on accommodations. The result was that the whole of Flagstaff responded by digging in deep and finding the needed resources. Meals, rooms, toiletries and incidentals that had been forgotten in the haste to get there—the town tried to provide for all those streaming in. Tribal leaders issued a Sympathy Resolution at the traditional breakfast meetup before kicking off the Pow Wow festivities. The national press that descended on the town brought plenty of publicity, but the people turned their attention to the victims' families. They jumped in to help in whatever ways they could, and by all accounts the town conducted itself admirably and with compassion.

As the planes and choppers flew in with their cargo of black rubber bags, it became evident that little remained of the passengers. In the end, Flagstaff received a total of twenty-eight bags from both the TWA and United sites. On July 9, a mass funeral was held for all those who died in the collision. Twenty-nine unidentified victims of United 718 were placed in four coffins and interred at the Grand Canyon Pioneer Cemetery. Sixty-six of the passengers and crew from TWA 2 were buried in a mass grave at the eastern edge of Citizens Cemetery, their names engraved on a bronze plaque set into a slab of granite. The grave site is unique—a large, raised rectangular plot of grass with a low stone wall surrounding the area. Throughout the years, family members and sympathetic visitors have left painted rocks, old photographs, letters and other mementos on the step next to the passengers' names. It's a quiet, peaceful place on the gentle rise of the cemetery, with a serenity that belies the Constellation's tragic end.

The public outcry after the crash was immediate and loud, but it took several more years before federal reforms to the commercial airline industry were in place. Today, a pilot cannot deviate from his or her designated flight plan to give passengers a peek at a national monument. Radar, instrument-controlled flying, black boxes and advanced technology at every level have made air travel safer than driving a car. The passenger *experience* has suffered; instead of a four-course meal, one is lucky to get a bag of peanuts. That, however, has more to do with industry profit than the FAC and ATC reforms.

The TWA mass grave in Citizens Cemetery is also a memorial to those whose lives were lost. Friends and family members visit and leave tributes. *Author's collection.*

In researching the TWA Flight 2 memorial, I came across anecdotes and bits of trivia I hadn't heard before. Some of the stories are heartbreaking: the bride-to-be who didn't make it to her wedding, the thoughtless remark to a spouse that couldn't be taken back, the daughter who missed hugging her father goodbye that fateful morning and other sad remembrances. An excellent book written by Mike Nelson, *We Are Going In: The Story of the 1956 Grand Canyon Midair Collision*, gives a complete account of the day and its aftermath. Nelson's uncle was on United 718, and his book is hailed as being both heartfelt and technical. The author holds slightly different opinions than other sources I've found, but his book is carefully researched. For example, Nelson believes both pilots caught sight of each other in the final seconds before impact. He came to this conclusion through countless re-creations of the collision using the angle at which they collided. He also asserts that, while the DC-7's left wing sliced through the TWA tail, the reverse was true as well. Aerodynamically, the Super-Connie tore through approximately one-third of United's left wing. While this may seem trivial, it is a different way to look at the accident. Nelson writes that it's likely Captain Shirley was not at the controls when the collision occurred; rather, he believes it's probable he was back in the cabin, greeting the passengers. Nelson spoke extensively to aviation experts and actual first-responders to the accident sites. He backs up his theories with plenty of math and input from the experts whom he consulted.

A report issued in 1957 included details of a federal agency's search for eyewitnesses. Officials traveled to the Navajo Reservation and questioned several residents about what they might have seen that day. Later, the same investigators contacted Grand Canyon Park visitors who had driven in or were staying there on June 30. These investigators searched in vain for months; no one, it seems, saw the two planes collide—at least, no one the board found credible. The following is text taken from the National Transportation Safety Board's (NTSB) report on the accident, published April 17, 1957:

> *An exhaustive search for eyewitnesses to the inflight collision was conducted. Many persons were contacted in the popular tourist area, as were employees of the Grand Canyon Park Service and residents of the surrounding area. During this search no witnesses were found who saw the collision although at least one person apparently saw smoke from the crashes and dismissed it....Later, on July 10, two witnesses were made known to the Board and were called to appear at the public hearing. These witnesses stated that while driving west on Route 66 between Winona and Flagstaff they saw the two aircraft collide. Their description fitted the subject aircraft and especially the Constellation. Both witnesses stated that when the collision occurred there was no evidence such as fire, smoke, or falling pieces and that following impact the aircraft seemed to continue on without falling but locked together.*[62]

The board found these eyewitnesses' testimony questionable and reinterviewed them more thoroughly. Investigators also duplicated the couple's drive from Winona and concluded it would have been impossible to see the aircraft. The report stated that they did not doubt the witnesses' sincerity, but several other airplanes in the sky that day might have confused the couple.

A third witness came forward and reported having seen smoke in the area of the Grand Canyon that day. This man was also driving west on Route

The rustic El Tovar Hotel sits precariously close to the south rim. No one at the canyon that July morning reported seeing the collision. *Library of Congress, Historic American Buildings Survey.*

66 at the time although he was closer to Winslow. The board conceded the smoke might have been from the collision, but there was not enough information to be certain.

The most interesting witness to step forward waited until February 1, 1957, to do so. The board was just about to publish its report but delayed the long-awaited paper and took the man's deposition:

> *In Substance, the witness testified that on June 30, 1956, while proceeding to the Grand Canyon, he made his observations through the windshield of a Ford pickup truck in which he was traveling alone on Route 64 toward Desert View at a speed of 75–80 miles an hour up a prolonged incline in the road. At the point of observation he was between 5 and 7 miles south of Desert View or 15–17 miles south of the estimated collision point.*
>
> *When questioned as to why he did not make public the fact that he had observed the accident, he answered that he did not want to embarrass himself.…The Board has carefully evaluated all of the testimony of this witness and concluded that it has no probative value. First, we cannot accept the witness' statement with regard to weather conditions.…Second, with respect to the witness' description of the relative positions and identification*

of the aircraft, it is unlikely that the witness could have seen these aircraft in the manner and from the place he described.

The NTSB report goes on in great detail, giving weather conditions, angles of trajectory and more to support its conclusion that the witness was unreliable. What it did not indicate in that report was the testimony that the man gave. I believe it's likely the man was Fred Riley, who gave an interview to *LIFE* magazine in 1959 regarding what he saw that day. The following is an excerpt from that article:

Riley, a phenomenally taciturn man, had been driving along a road near the canyon rim when through his windshield he noticed two planes perhaps 10 miles directly ahead of him. For a moment Riley took his eyes off the planes. When he looked again the two silhouettes had, astonishingly, merged. He demonstrated with his hands. "This plane here"—he gesticulated—"peeled right off and went over like this....It looked to me like it had bent, like this—broken....It didn't glide at all; it tipped over and went right straight down. The other took off in a gliding angle....It looked like it possibly kept on the same general flight, and then it tipped over and went down."

The puzzled examiners asked Riley why he had not come forth with his story sooner. At first, he explained, he had thought the collision was a hallucination—a visual trick played by the shimmering heat. He had not reported it because he was afraid of being laughed at. Later, he had found everybody too busy. "I didn't want to, you know, bring anything up that might unduly upset you people, you see, in your investigation, because there is always plenty of time for me to talk to you....If it was a question of a month, six months or a year, you see, I could still come back and tell you what I saw."[63]

The NTSB's final report stated there were no credible witnesses to the tragedy of June 30, 1956. The conclusion they reached as to the cause of the collision was so simple as to be taken as insulting by the public: the pilots failed to see one another. However, as one looks back from today, it's as good a reason as another that was put forth: perhaps it was fate. From the series of choices made by the LAX ground crew before takeoff that had the planes depart precisely when they did to the many decisions made by each pilot in air as they changed course and altered altitude, every action led to this disastrous end. In a wide-open, partly cloudy sky over one of the wonders of the world, 128 souls departed this earth. It's still a lot to fathom.

The crash of '56 has become part of canyon lore, especially with hikers and river runners sitting around a camp stove. Many of these stories center on the canyon floor closest to the crash sites. One has a ranger awakening in her tent to the sound of footsteps and whisperings around 2:00 a.m. When she stuck her head out to look, she saw a long line of people hiking single-file up from the river. Some of the women were in dresses and heels, totally inappropriate for walking this remote area of the canyon. As they neared her tent, the ranger realized that the people didn't even see her. She pulled her head back inside and curled up in her sleeping bag. Another story from *A Journey Into the Haunted* details the sighting of people dressed in "city clothes" wandering the rocky canyon floor between the two crash sites. As the hikers drew closer, there were no people—no living people—to be seen. Oddly, I've not heard of any ghostly appearances at the TWA Memorial in Citizens Cemetery.[64]

There are many aspects to this horrific tragedy that are legitimately "wicked," including the FAC's slow response to increased air travel and the hand of fate behind the fatal choices that day. However, what was really ugly was the public outcry for a scapegoat. This tragedy remained in the national news for weeks, and the search was on for someone to blame. There were, of course, the pilots, both of whom altered their courses to give passengers a scenic thrill. It was TWA's Jack Gandy who took the brunt of the public's scorn, probably because of poor communications from the Civil Aeronauts Board at the time. The blame shifted as pictures and information were released to an ill-informed press, most of who didn't understand the aviation field. The Flight Dispatch Centers and ATC in Utah also came under fire, as if the staff wanted to steer two planes into each other! After a thorough investigation, all of these entities were cleared of any responsibility for the collision. Those findings wouldn't be published until April 1957, though, well after angry accusations had been thrown around publicly. In his book *We Are Going In*, Mike Nelson gives awful accounts of the shame that dogged the professionals and family members of people involved in the accident.

Looking through past issues of the *Daily Sun* reveals very little condemnation coming from Flagstaff. Possibly because the town had been in the thick of the post-collision activity, locals could put some of the faces and names together. Or perhaps the town had a more accurate view of the accident and how incomprehensible the whole tragedy was. For whatever reason, Flagstaff stood tall in the aftermath and didn't involve itself in any of the widespread pettiness. Survivors of the victims have returned here throughout the decades to visit the grave sites. When interviewed by the press, they've expressed gratitude for the community that provided comfort and aid in their time of need.

THE SKINWALKER
MURDER TRIAL

urprisingly underreported, given the defense's flamboyant strategy, the 1987 murder of Sarah Saganitso remains unsolved to this day. I have my thoughts on why this wicked crime and the ensuing trial are relatively unknown, which I share later in the chapter. However, this tragic story is both fascinating and unique in the way it unfolded, both before the trial and in the courtroom.[65]

June 12, 1987, was another lovely summer's evening in Flagstaff. That Friday night, forty-year-old Sarah Louise Saganitso was finishing her first swing shift at Flagstaff Medical Center (FMC). Sarah had worked at FMC in the housekeeping department for the past seventeen years but had always worked the morning shift. The new schedule brought different responsibilities, and Saganitso had taken classes in the weeks before to prepare for the changes. By all accounts the evening went smoothly and without any incidents. Sarah was reportedly seen at 10:45 p.m. near the employee timeclock by one of her coworkers, and nothing appeared to be amiss. That, however, was the last time the hospital worker was seen alive by anyone except her killer.

Sarah Saganitso was born in Tuba City on the Navajo Nation in August 1947. She came from a large, close-knit Navajo family with seven brothers and seven sisters. She moved to Flagstaff in 1966 and found work in various healthcare positions until settling in with FMC sometime in 1970. Sarah lived in town in a trailer with her four-year-old son, Alvin, whom she was raising alone. She was known to be a devoted single mother and a

This trail, roughly 100 yards south of the hospital, leads into the woods to where Saganitso's body was found. *Author's collection.*

dependable, quiet coworker. Sarah was well liked at the hospital, and no one there had a bad word to say about her.

Saganitso did not return home that night after her shift was over. Since this was her first evening shift, there might have been some confusion over when she was due in. However, it soon became clear that something was wrong; Sarah was not irresponsible, and she wouldn't have disappeared for a night on the town. As the minutes ticked by and turned into hours, her family became worried and called up to the hospital. When it was confirmed that she had clocked out at 11:00 p.m., family members drove up to FMC to look for her. They found Saganitso's truck in the parking lot but no Sarah. There was one odd bit of circumstance—a clump of dirt sat on the asphalt near the driver's door, looking very out of place. But that was it—no blood and no signs of a struggle near the truck.

Her family checked inside the hospital, but no one there knew anything about Sarah's whereabouts after she clocked out. The Flagstaff Police Department was notified, and Saturday morning they initiated a formal search. A few of Saganitso's coworkers joined in, scouring the forests north and southwest of FMC. It was in a rocky, wooded area only one hundred yards southwest of the parking lot that one of them made a gruesome discovery. Among the debris behind the A.J. Bayless store lay a woman's badly beaten body. It was Sarah Saganitso, naked and covered in her own blood. She had obviously been dead for some hours.

The hospital worker's murder was headline news for the week following her death. As said before, she was known for being a quiet, responsible woman, and everyone who knew her was shocked. The first report was that Saganitso had been stabbed multiple times in the chest; however, the official finding was death by suffocation. It appeared her killer had held a hand over the woman's mouth and nose, cutting off her airway. The copious amount of blood found at the murder scene came from cuts or bite marks and from Saganitso being beaten. Besides her clothing, some of her personal effects were also missing, including an ID badge, prescription glasses and a purse. It appeared that the perpetrator who brutalized Sarah had also kicked sticks and grass over her upper torso. There were other oddities about the scene that would come out later, but in the weeks after the crime, the police went silent. To all outside appearances, the case had gone cold.[66]

Then on September 2, 1987, the community awoke to a startling headline in the *Daily Sun*: "Police Arrest Suspect in June Murder." The front-page article was accompanied by the image of a somewhat handsome if ragged-looking man identified as George William Abney. The initial report on

Sarah's accused murderer was brief and contained several errors, one being that Abney was a transient. However, many articles were to follow, and soon the community had a clearer picture of who the suspect was.[67]

It turned out that George Abney was a thirty-five-year-old veteran of both the U.S. Air Force and the Naval Reserves. He came to Flagstaff sometime around 1982 to attend graduate school at Northern Arizona University. After receiving his master's degree, Abney taught freshman English classes at the university and moonlighted at several local hotels. He had been renting a house close to the hospital in June 1987 and lived there with at least one roommate. According to police, a week after Sarah's body was discovered, Abney packed his belongings and left for South Carolina, where his parents lived. While his departure was abrupt, it wasn't totally spontaneous. Abney had told friends that he'd applied for a job in China teaching English. In the meantime, he said, he'd decided to move east and wait out an answer while staying with his folks.

As the story began to unfold, though, it was evident it was more complicated than he'd initially made out. The former teacher had made

Disturbing dream led police to a suspect

BY STEVE RYAN
Sun Staff Reporter

George Abney actually was telling police about a disturbing dream during the portion of a videotape which was "artfully" portrayed as a murder confession during a presentation which caused grand jurors to charge Abney with killing a hospital maid, alleges Abney's attorney.

Viewing the tape and other records of Abney's statements would reveal that Abney was, during the period interviews were taped, a young man "very disturbed by a dream that bothered him," in part because Abney's religious orientation attaches significance to dreams, attorney Harold Watkins said during a court hearing today.

Abney became a suspect in the slaying of 40-year-old Sara Saganitso only after the dream disturbed him to the point that he sought counseling from his minister, "who just happened to be Det. Blair's father-in-law, who then related it to" Jerry Blair, a detective with the Flagstaff Police Department, Watkins alleged. "That got this whole thing started."

Blair reportedly also is a member of the Flagstaff

detectives who interviewed Abney several times in the course of the investigation, Watkins alleged during today's hearing.

Abney became confused during the course of the investigation and for a time he came to consider himself a possible suspect in the case, according to Atha.

Minister Dave Patterson, who began counseling Abney four days after the arrest of Abney Sept. 1, said Abney's rationale when he considered himself a suspect was that police told Abney they had accumulated substantial evidence against him.

"There was a lot of confusion; he would constantly relate back to the evidence police told him they have," said Dave Patterson.

However, Abney's independent recollection of the dreams initially was inconsistent with facts of the Saganitso case, including the description of Saganitso, said Dave Patterson.

Abney now has resolved his doubts and he believes that he has been falsely accused, according to Atha.

A friend of Abney, 28-year-old Guillermo Vasquez, said he was with Abney beginning no later than 11:30 p.m. at a motel across town from the murder site on the

The *Daily Sun* closely followed the Saganitso murder case, reporting on the court proceedings. *Courtesy of the* Arizona Daily Sun.

disturbing statements to several people over the past months. To begin with, one of Abney's friends said the instructor was "obsessed" with Saganitso's murder in the week before he left. Now, the whole community was taken with the tragedy, and it was the subject of many conversations. There was a great deal of trepidation in town over the killer being at large. Female staff at the hospital were being escorted to their cars after work. So the fact that Abney was also talking about Sarah's death doesn't seem abnormal. However, he claimed to some friends he'd begun to have disturbing dreams about a Hispanic man murdering a woman "up by the hospital." Abney stated these nightmares had started a few weeks before the murder occurred. They continued to plague him after he'd left Flagstaff, to a point where he wasn't sleeping and feared he was heading for a nervous breakdown.

Abney's lawyer later said his client's religion put great stock in prophetic dreams, so when the murder actually occurred, he was shocked and frightened. The attorney also implied that this was the reason behind Abney's sudden move to South Carolina. According to Abney, as the dreams continued unabated, he'd begun to doubt his own sanity. He moved back to Arizona, albeit to Sierra Vista, to seek answers.

During the six or seven years the English major lived here, he was a member of the Flagstaff Tabernacle Church. When Abney returned to Arizona, he phoned his former minister, Floyd Patterson, and sought counseling. According to news accounts, Abney was very disturbed by the ongoing dreams and told Patterson he was having difficulty separating these visions from reality. In fact, it appeared he was fearful that he *might* have been the murderer that night. Abney was so upset and confused that he told Patterson he was going to sign himself into a "mental hospital." However, a new twist now entered into what was becoming a truly bizarre tale.

Apparently unknown to George Abney, Pastor Patterson was the father-in-law of Flagstaff detective Jerry Blair. It seems Patterson was able to convince Abney to stay put long enough for the minister to contact members of the Flag PD. The minister relayed his concerns over the man's possible confession to the detectives working the case. Whether a small contingency of law enforcement traveled to Sierra Vista or contact was made via phone, the result was that Abney voluntarily returned to Flagstaff. He was interrogated for over ten hours—much of it taped—at the station. Then on September 1, 1987, Abney was charged with the first-degree murder of Sarah Saganitso.

The community was both relieved that the killer was off the streets and perturbed as more details became known. Several of Abney's former NAU colleagues and students expressed disbelief at his arrest. While some admitted the man could be odd, no one thought he was a murderer. The September 3, 1987 *Sun* reported:

> *According to Dr. Paul J. Ferlazzo, chairman of the NAU English Department, Abney graduated from NAU with a master's degree in English in 1986 and taught as a teacher's assistant at the university for two years. "He was a quiet man, a conscientious teacher....Reports are he was a good student, he met his classes, he had friends on the staff." One of Abney's former students said, "I thought he was a little strange. He was a fairly good teacher, but he told strange stories about his childhood during class."*

The *Lumberjack*, NAU's student newspaper, ran an article echoing the same sentiments.

As the case was being built against the former instructor, more troubling news was leaked to the public. Depending on which side one believed, Abney was either a deranged killer or a confused, sick man being scapegoated by the police. The taped confession, which was played during the 1988 trial, appeared to show signs of both. It became known that Patterson and Detective Blair were both present at various times during the interrogation process, and it was speculated that they were feeding Abney information. This would culminate in trial testimony by a mind-control expert, Dr. Richard Ofshe, regarding the mechanics of false confessions.

There was also the evidence provided by two forensic odontologists—bite-mark specialists. This was fairly new science in the late 1980s, and even the prosecution admitted the accuracy rate for matching teeth marks was 67 percent at best. However, they persisted in calling the patterns "evidence," so the defense brought in two forensic pathologists of their own. Their experts disputed that the wounds on Sarah's torso were from teeth; rather, they believed the marks were from some kind of pointed tool. Regardless, there was a clip of George Abney on tape admitting he bit Sarah:

Bite mark key to murder case

BY STEVE RYAN
Sun Staff Reporter

The bite mark evidence was both new and highly controversial in the trial.
Courtesy of the Arizona Daily Sun.

After being told by investigators that his teeth matched the wound, Abney allegedly told investigators that the bite mark was a "signature" he left so he could be identified, Thompson said.

Bruce Griffen, one of Abney's defense attorneys, knew that his client had dug himself into a deep hole during that ten-hour interrogation. He attempted to plant reasonable doubt in the public's mind through pretrial interviews:

Investigators, over the course of more than 10 hours of interrogation and with the assistance from the minister, asked "leading questions and planted suggestions" to extract erroneous statements from the "vulnerable" Abney, alleged Griffen….Statements by Abney are unsupported by evidence in the case….Abney allegedly told investigators that he was denied treatment at the hospital and that Saganitso subsequently drove him to the Sportsman Bar, where they stayed for a short time before stopping at the Cork and Bottle liquor store and returning to the hospital area. However, nobody at the hospital, at the bar or at the liquor store recalled seeing Abney on the night of the slaying, said Griffen.[68]

The trial began almost a year to the date of Sarah's murder. While the preceding information might have some readers shaking their heads, it was the defense's strategy that made this trial one for the books. The defendant who walked into court on June 16, 1988, looked much calmer and more together than the man who appeared on the tape. One thing was certain—George Abney no longer believed he killed Sarah Saganitso. Before jury selection commenced, both sides laid out their basic premises. That was when the defense dropped its bombshell: George Abney did not kill Sarah Saganitso—a Navajo Skinwalker did.

Before going further, it might help to define a Skinwalker, also known as Yenaldlooshi, because descriptions vary depending on the source. Abney's defense attorneys hired an expert witness, Utah State folklore professor Barre Toelken, to present evidence that suggested the involvement of witchcraft in Sarah's murder. Toelken consulted with author Margaret Brady in a book, *Some Kind of Power*, in which the following description appears:

Navajo traditional belief clearly indicates that yenaldlooshi meet in caves at night to initiate these new members, as well as to plan concerted action against victims, to have intercourse with the dead and to practice

The Navajo Reservation is colorful and desolate. At nighttime, many people keep their doors locked and drapes drawn to rebuff the supernatural. *Photo by Paul F. Jones circa 1984, Author's collection.*

> *cannibalism.…Perhaps the most significant aspect of the skinwalker's animal like behavior is the very skin he dons, a change that literally as well as symbolically transforms him from human to animal.….Navajo skinwalkers constantly move between the world of humans and animals, throwing the two differing domains together, contrasting them and somehow almost making them equal to each other once again.*

Brady and others assert that Yenaldlooshi often assume the shape of a coyote. Most Navajo will not utter the name of the feared shapeshifter, as they do not want to attract the Skinwalker's attention.

Another definition of a Skinwalker comes from the *Legends of America* blog article "Navajo Skinwalkers—Witches of the Southwest." It's a good description and more in line with what I've heard from those few willing to discuss this entity:

> *In the Navajo culture, a skinwalker is a type of harmful witch who has the ability to turn into, possess, or disguise themselves as an animal. This witch is called "yee naaldlooshi" by the Navajo, which translates to "with it, he goes on all fours." It is just one of several types of Navajo witches and is considered to be the most volatile and dangerous.*

In this article, Kathy Alexander goes on to describe the traditional Navajo way, which includes magic of all kinds and from many sources. Medicine men traditionally use their powers to harness this spiritual energy for the benefit of those seeking their help. Those who practice "Witchery Way," however, direct the energy to harm others. Alexander continues in her writings to describe who and what a skinwalker is:

> *Though they can be either male or female, they are most often male. They walk freely among the tribe during the day and secretly transform under the cover of night. To become a Skinwalker, he or she must be initiated by a secret society that requires the evilest of deeds—the killing of a close family member, most often a sibling....They are often seen as coyotes, wolves, foxes, cougars, dogs and bears, but they can take the shape of any animal.*

Besides transforming into a predatory animal, Alexander writes that the entity has other frightening powers:

> *The skinwalkers can also take possession of the bodies of human victims if a person locks eyes with them. After taking control, the witch can make its victims do and say things they wouldn't otherwise. Once they were shape-shifted, others could tell they were not real animals because their eyes were very different from those of the animals. Instead, their eyes are very human....Alternatively, their eyes look more like animals when they are in human form.*

Alexander's article is quite long and fascinatingly detailed. I read many descriptions and stories about Navajo Skinwalkers for this chapter, and hers is one of the clearest. One other bit of information she shares is something I've been told by friends and relatives who've spent time on the reservation. Skinwalkers have many superpowers, including the ability to outrun a car cruising along a dark highway. When glimpsed by an unfortunate Anglo, they often appear as a dark, shadowy, not-quite-human form loping alongside their vehicle. Then, in a nearly impossible feat of acrobatic agility, the figure will leap ahead and disappear into the surrounding land. I've heard these sightings recounted in hushed tones by engineers, teachers and other individuals who swear they've experienced something terrifying and supernatural in the night.

Back to the trial. The prosecution went first and brought several witnesses who stated Abney had been seen lurking about the hospital in the weeks before Saganitso's murder. Friends of Abney's were also questioned about his whereabouts that night. All in all, that evidence against him seemed weak. Two of his buddies swore Abney was with them, playing pool or drinking at the time of Sarah's murder. Then the prosecutor played the ten-plus-hour interrogation tape in which the defendant went back and forth, confessing, recanting and never answering simple questions about how the murder was done. Later in the trial, the prosecution's forensic odontologist testified that Abney's teeth were a definite match to the bitemarks on Sarah's torso and left nipple. This testimony was crucial, as there was no other direct evidence—no fingerprints, no blood, no hair—that linked the defendant to the crime scene.

The defense countered the prosecution's evidence and then, on July 7, Professor Toelken took the stand. It was at this time that the highly unusual and ritualistic features of the crime were revealed in the courtroom. According to testimony, the body was found with a stick carefully placed across Saganitso's throat. Toelken said this was indicative of witchcraft, as Navajos associate the cutting off of a person's breath with killing their spirit. A broken stick, like one at the crime scene, was another aspect of Navajo ritual slaying, as was a cut shaped like a crescent-moon found near her left breast. The tip of Sarah's left breast had been removed and was possibly missing. She was found nude, and her personal effects were not at the crime scene. Toelken said witches often buried such items—jewelry, glasses and so on—in the graves of other victims to cause confusion and pain to surviving relatives. And remember that clump of dirt found on the parking lot pavement next to Sarah's truck? Toelken testified that this was likely cemetery grass and was meant as a warning to family members against pursing an investigation.

The prosecution cross-examined Dr. Toelken and made a few points. As the trial proceeded, the forensic odontologists' evidence proved to be a wash. Both sides provided experts that contradicted the other, and the most that could be said was that no saliva was recovered from any of the "bite marks." However, another odd piece of evidence was the discovery of two animal hairs found inside the deceased's mouth and inside the breast wound. While the defense claimed this supported the Skinwalker theory, they had to concede there were plenty of small animals in the woods where Saganitso's body was found. Abney's attorneys also raised the question of whether Sarah's former boyfriend, a Navajo man who had been abusive to her in the past, was involved. While the man had submitted his blood and fingerprints, his alibi for the night in question was shaky.

George Abney did not testify in his own behalf. When the case went to the jury on Tuesday, July 19, the nine-man, three-woman panel deliberated for less than four hours. They came back with a verdict of not guilty and the defendant was set free. Members of Sarah's large family had been a presence in the courtroom, and they were there for the verdict. They embraced the defendant, with her brother-in-law saying:

> *The trial is over now, but there is a new beginning we must look forward to. We must start to work together and bring out the truth. On the way, we met a new friend we never heard of. I hope he forgives us for what many observers thought he was the one. My friends, he is innocent.*

For their part, the Flagstaff Police Department considered the case closed. There would be no further investigation into Saganitso's death, as they felt the killer had just gotten away with murder.[69]

Jury takes little time in setting George Abney free

The Saganitso family stood behind Abney after hearing the evidence presented at court. *Courtesy of the* Arizona Daily Sun.

There are so many questions that come to mind when one takes a look at this sadly fascinating case. To begin with, the mechanics of that night were never adequately explained. Saganitso was last seen at the time clock, ready to end her "first-ever" swing shift in her seventeen years at FMC. Some find the shift change significant and theorize that it may be related to her tragic death. I'm curious about how and where Saganitso was abducted. Did she walk alone to her truck that night and someone was hiding inside or nearby? How was it that at end of shift, no one saw her after she left the building? It seems improbable she was the only employee walking to the parking lot after work. Perhaps she wasn't violently abducted at all; her killer might have been someone she thought of as a friend. No screams were reported that clear summer's night. Sarah's sister testified that about four days before the murder, Sarah admitted that she was afraid but then didn't explain further. The whole night after 11:00 p.m. is shrouded in mystery. Saganitso was known as a devoted mother, loving sister and reliable, conscientious employee; everyone who knew her said she'd never go off after work without notifying her son's sitter.

I wrote at the beginning of this story that I had a theory about why this unusual trial went relatively unnoticed. Sadly, it's because of another tragedy that occurred in town the summer of 1988. On Sunday June 5, Nancy Wilson drove from Yuma with her four young children to meet her husband, Richard, in Flagstaff. The family was looking forward to spending the summer in the mountains while Richard, a contractor, completed a project. On Monday, Nancy took her children with her as she transported the family's horses to a nearby ranch. Nine-year-old Jennifer asked her mother if she could ride her bike to the stables and meet them all there. With her mother's permission, the carefree little girl took off toward the barns, getting a head start. At that time, Peaceful Valley Road was little more than a graded dirt lane that eventually ended near Walnut Canyon. It was by no means a heavily traveled route. As Nancy Wilson pulled the horse trailer the short distance to the ranch, a truck roared past her, careening recklessly. As she drove farther up the road, Wilson came upon a sight that no mother wants to see. Off to the side on the shoulder was Jennifer's bicycle, twisted and bent as if hit by a vehicle. There was, however, no sign of the nine-year-old.

The abduction of Jennifer Wilson set off one of the largest manhunts ever conducted in northern Arizona, with local officials, search and rescue, the Marines and others arriving to help. Police had their suspicions, and a twenty-six-year-old local man, Ricky Bible, was held in jail on charges of auto theft. Bible had recently been released from prison after serving time for rape and he'd been seen in the area where Jennifer went missing. However, Bible wasn't talking, and for the next twenty days, television reports and newspaper articles kept the public apprised of the search efforts. When Abney's trial commenced, the two stories shared front-page space in the *Daily Sun*. The Wilsons' tragic vigil ended on June 25 when two hikers going up Sheep's Hill in east Flagstaff discovered the little girl's shoes and clothing. Jennifer's badly beaten body was found atop the hill, close to where Bible had committed another rape years earlier. Richard Bible was tried and convicted of the little girl's death. He was executed on June 30, 2011, by lethal injection.

Jennifer's abduction and the search that followed consumed the public's attention, just as Sarah's murder had the previous year. Sadly, as the Wilson parents noted in a later interview, the victim is too soon forgotten once a perpetrator has been found. This change in focus is how our legal system is set up; the court case concentrates on the accused while the victim is relegated to the periphery. Both of these senseless killings affected the town deeply, leaving their marks on those who lived here. They were a heartbreaking reminder that wickedness can rear its fearful head when least expected, even in an idyllic mountain oasis.

NOTES

Introduction

1. As I found in writing my first two books for The History Press, Flagstaff's Walkup Family Tragedy and Haunted Flagstaff, when it comes to detailing northern Arizona's beginnings, sources often run together. Platt Cline—late reporter, editor and publisher of the *Arizona Daily Sun*—is fondly acknowledged as the town's chief historian. However, even he quoted liberally from area newspapers such as the *Champion* and the *Coconino Sun* (always citing his sources, of course!). All this is to say that descriptions and information found in the introduction come from multiple sources that are difficult to untangle and may be found in pages within the bibliography.

2. Zane Grey frequented the area and often stayed at the Weatherford Hotel in rooms that were renovated into today's Zane Grey Ballroom. He's been widely credited with popularizing the Canyonlands. When young people look blank at the mention of his name, I ask them to think of an author with the status of Stephen King.

Chapter 1

3. Hudson, "Towns of the Western Railroads," 41–54. This is a fascinating look at the economic strategy behind the railroad's choice of townsites and the subsequent interplay between the corporation and the people. Hudson ascribed the quote to an unnamed source in a *Harper's Magazine* article.

4. Shock, "History of Flagstaff."

5. While Platt Cline quoted the *Coconino Sun* article in his book *Mountain Town*, the stories are taken from the July 11, 1895 edition of the newspaper. Those "tales" not cited to the newspaper are found in chapter 2 of Cline's book.

6. There are many sources that tell the story of Coconino County's creation, particularly Platt Cline's *Mountain Town*, of course, scattered throughout chapter 2. Wikipedia also has detailed recaps of the Arizona Territorial Legislative sessions, where much of the early business of creating counties, laws and preparing for statehood took place.

7. Cline, *Mountain Town*, 43.

8. Ibid., chapter 2. Information also supplemented with various issues of the *Coconino Sun*.

Chapter 2

9. In the Detour Effect website article "Folklore, Legends, and Mysteries of Flagstaff, Arizona," the reader can find all kinds of obscure stories on the people and events that shaped this town, as well as tales of lost treasure, murder and ghostly hauntings. This is the first site I found that dubbed Commodore Perry Owens the "Fabio of the West." The background information I gathered on Owens came from multiple sources. It would be impossible to untangle the various threads, as most of them agree with one another. Differing accounts arise after Owens settled in Navajo Springs. Credit goes to thedetoureffect.com; the podcasts Wild West Extravaganza (June 14, 21) and True Stories of the Old West (April 18, 2022); Wikipedia; True West magazine (August 10, 2021); and Kathy Alexander's article on the Legends of America website, "Commodore Perry Owens—Gunfighting Lawman," November 2022, www.legendsofamerica.com.

10. Details of Owens's escapades in Navajo Springs and as Apache County sheriff are described in detail in the historical article "Commodore Perry Owens Helped Clean Up Early Years of Apache County" by Jack Becker, which can be read on roundvalleyaz.com. It includes clips from several old newspapers, including the *Apache County Critic*, the *St. John's Herald* and summaries from the *Tucson Citizen*. The quotes regarding Owens's showdown with Blevins come from this article. The *Wild West Extravaganza* podcast also put out an entertaining yet accurate episode on Owens and expounded on the many controversies behind the man as he straddled the changing times.

11. Owens's showdown with Blevins and gang is an infamous episode in the notorious Pleasant Valley War saga. The Navajo County Historical Museum is located

inside the county courthouse in Holbrook, where the gunfight took place. The museum is free and holds many remnants from decades past; however, there's not as much history on the Owens-Blevins shootout. The old Blevins house sits a few blocks away and is now a nursing home or extended care facility. Its infamy is noted only by a weathered sign.

12. Cline, *They Came to the Mountain*, 221.

Chapter 3

13. I thought hard about writing the last sentence, as I've found no documentation of a "money scandal" involving the cemeteries. However, enough people mentioned it ("it" being that old graves were dug up, the remains disposed of and the newly dead interred in their place) that I had to mention it. Again, no evidence.

14. Cline, *They Came to the Mountain*, chapter 11.

15. Joe Meehan is a local historian who is well-versed in most everything Flagstaff, including the old cemeteries. He helped put together the fundraising cemetery tours and has been generous in sharing information about where the bodies are buried, so to speak.

16. Cline, *Mountain Town*, 95.

17. *Flagstaff's Walkup Family Murders: A Shocking 1937 Tragedy* was my first book for The History Press. Very little is known about why Marie committed these terrible acts, although she left several notes behind. In one she asked her husband to keep the funeral services private, which he did. The *Coconino Sun* reported that locals lined the streets to pay their respects as the hearses drove past.

18. *Coconino Sun*, April 6, 1906.

19. NAU Ice Hockey, nauhockey.com; Jay Lively, 1967–1984.

20. Doney's antics were peppered throughout the *Coconino Sun*. There are plenty of papers, articles and historical anecdotes about him online, which seem to have drawn the same conclusion I did.

21. Background information on Calvary Cemetery was found online at Catholic Cemeteries & Funeral Homes, *Mountain Town* by Platt Cline and "Who Lies Beneath," the Calvary Catholic Cemetery Tour put together as a fundraiser for the Northern Arizona Pioneer's Historical Society, October 8, 2017.

22. The story of the unfortunate William Lamb and the Hawk brothers' lynching is told in Platt Cline's *They Came to the Mountain*, chapter 11, pages 297–99.

23. *Coconino Sun*, January 27, 1911.

Chapter 4

24. These various facts can be found throughout Cline's Mountain Town. Cline also included appendices; Appendix C is a list of Yavapai and Coconino County officials dating from 1882 and running through 1992. The book's Appendix D lists Flagstaff town and city officials dating from 1894.

25. Much of this chapter's information, unless otherwise cited, came from reports from the Arizona Territorial Assemblies. They can be found in abbreviated form on Wikipedia by entering the specific session or in full on the Arizona Memory Project. Northern Arizona University also has a page dedicated to its early history, where other bits of information can be found.

26. Cline, *Mountain Town*, 62–63. Cline's accurate yet abbreviated version of the town dodging the assembly can be found on these pages.

Chapter 5

27. As one might expect, Platt Cline faithfully details the evolution of the *Arizona Champion* to the *Coconino Sun* to the *Arizona Daily Sun* in both of his books (*They Came to the Mountain* and *Mountain Town*). A supplemental resource I used was Donald Shock's 1952 thesis, "The History of Flagstaff." I relied on all three sources, as it could be confusing to follow who was writing and/or owned the local paper and when it morphed into another entity.

28. *Coconino Sun Weekly*, January 4, 1894.

29. *Coconino Sun Weekly*, January 25, 1894.

30. Ibid.

31. Ibid.

32. These ads, as well as the list of local fraternities, ran in almost every *Coconino Sun Weekly* until the turn of the century. They often used the same people/names and made a story out of cataloguing their woes. I'll add that the few examples in this chapter not cited with a date were clipped examples from the *Coconino Sun Weekly*.

33. *Arizona Daily Sun*, May 5, 1948.

34. *Arizona Daily Sun*, March 1948.

35. *Arizona Daily Sun*, January 4, 1949.

36. *Coconino Weekly Sun*, October 15, 1896.

37. Ibid., October 15, 1896.

38. *Coconino Sun*, June 18, 1898.

39. Ibid.

40. *Coconino Sun*, February 21, 1913.

41. *Coconino Sun*, March 21, 1919.

42. *Coconino Sun*, February 23, 1923.

43. *Coconino Sun*, January 25, 1918.

44. *Coconino Sun*, December 28, 1923.

45. *Coconino Sun*, January 5, 1923.

46. *Coconino Sun*, February 29, 1924.

47. *Coconino Sun*, February 1, 1924.

48. *Coconino Sun*, March 6, 1925.

49. *Coconino Sun*, February 27, 1925.

50. *Coconino Sun*, March 27, 1925.

51. *Coconino Sun*, April 10, 1925.

Chapter 6

52. I have cited sources for specific passages in this chapter and will make note of any as it proceeds. Much of my information came from the YouTube video, "The Forgotten Underground," the Weatherford Hotel's blog article "The Mystery of the Downtown Flagstaff 'Secret Underground Tunnels' Solved?"; Coveney, "Flagstaff's Tunnels Lead to a Mysterious Past"; personal interviews; and limited but actual exposure to the tunnel system.

53. Prejudice against Chinese people was a sad reality across the West in the late 1800s. I have taken specifics from the local papers (as cited), but there's a wealth of information online about this phenomenon. Like many prejudices, it was likely based on economic factors first, as the Chinese were seen as cheap labor for the railroad at the time. Chapter 9 of Cline's *They Came to the Mountain* details the town's abuse of the Chinese.

54. The three fires hold a special place in Flagstaff's history and are recounted in multiple sources. They are detailed completely in issues of the *Coconino Weekly Sun* and more succinctly by Platt Cline in his books.

55. Cline, *They Came to the Mountain*, 235.

56. The Sanborn Fire Insurance maps are another fascinating read for anyone interested in early American history. These maps were drawings of specific areas in towns across the United States and were used to assist fire insurance agents in assessing the degree of hazard in any particular building. They used color-coding for type of building construction (e.g. pink for brick, brown for adobe, blue for concrete) and had detailed legends showing locations of windows, recessed walls, chimneys, stoves and so forth. The Flagstaff maps, like other towns, were constructed and revised every so many years. They can be found online at the Library of Congress site. Interestingly, while they did have a code for "passageway," tunnels were not indicated on the maps.

Chapter 7

57. Almost all the hard information in this chapter came from the *Coconino Sun*, the September 1, 1916 and September 7, 1916 editions. However, I first heard of Dutch May and the mystery surrounding her unsolved murder while on a September 19, 2015 fundraiser for Northern Arizona Pioneer's Historical Society. This self-guided walking tour had the great name "Sinners, Saints, and Settlers" and had stops at the old brothels, gaming halls and churches south of the tracks. As usual, knowledgeable locals were stationed at each venue. The person sitting where Dutch's old shack had been was Joseph Jordan, the same man who first told me the story of the Walkup family tragedy. He shared a few educated opinions about Dutch and Mr. Prescott's demise with a group of us, which I've worked into the chapter.

58. The information on what became of May's properties comes from the booklet "Sinners, Saints, and Settlers: A Tour of Flagstaff's South Side." The story of Dutch and Mr. Prescott was told at the Grand Canyon Hostel stop.

Chapter 8

59. There's a tremendous amount of information online about the Grand Canyon air collision of 1956, and I've read a lot of it. Wikipedia gives a great overview, as does Admiral Cloudberg Medium article "Into the Abyss." Other great sources: Surette, "Story of the 1956 Grand Canyon Mid-Air Collision"; the Colorado Plateau Digital Collections within the NAU Library archives (which has black-and-white photos from the scene); *Mayday: The Grand Canyon Collision* (a TV show about airplane crashes); the podcast *Plane Crash Podcast*, March 25, 2021; and the book *We Are Going In* by Mike Nelson. These are just a few of the resources I've read and/or listened to about the tragedy, and I would recommend any of them. Nelson's book goes into the greatest depth on every aspect of the crash. He interviewed rescuers, family members, airline personnel and others who may have been more forthcoming with him because he lost an uncle who was on United 718.

60. Much is made over the fact that, minutes before takeoff at LAX, United 718 passed in front of the TWA plane to line itself up on runway 25L (left). TWA 2 was set to takeoff from runway 25R (right), which it did after the United plane crossed the lane and they were cleared by the control tower. In that minute it took for the airliners to get into their proper positions, when they crossed paths on the ground, the pilots and passengers of both would have been able to see one

another plainly through the windows. Did anyone experience a shiver of dread or premonition of the disaster that would occur less than three hours later? We can only imagine.

61. This communication in particular received a tremendous amount of attention—mostly negative—from the press and the public. While the Civil Aeronautics Board looked into it, as part of the investigation, the fateful radio exchange was dissected and replayed by television, newspapers, magazines and other outlets for months. The armchair investigators couldn't let go of the fact that (1) Captain Gandy flew his plane at twenty-one thousand feet under VFR rules, after first being denied the request; and (2) Utah ATC didn't advise the United flight that TWA was at the same altitude. However, it's important to note that all of this exchange between pilots and ATC was routine and legal under 1956 aviation laws. Gandy was allowed to request "1,000 on top," and he was given permission to ascend and advised of the United flight as his traffic. Utah ATC had no responsibility to babysit each and every pilot entering its airspace. There was no nationwide radar system in 1956; it was impossible to track exactly where each plane was and at what altitude with any certainty.

62. This report from the National Transportation Safety Board was released on April 17, 1957, and is sixty-two pages long. It can easily be found online with a simple Google search—I found it at fss.aero. While I'm excerpting sections regarding the search for eyewitnesses, the above is an in-depth report on the board's findings of the accident.

63. *LIFE* magazine, April 29, 1957

64. For more, see *Haunted Hikes* by Andrea Lankford. Lankford's book takes the reader on haunted trails throughout the United States. Her story about the ranger camped near the Colorado River is believable and spooky! Another great book is *Over the Edge: Death in Grand Canyon* by Michael P. Ghiglieri and Thomas M. Myers. This book has frightening tales of all too human nature but includes the crash of 1956. "A Journey into the Haunted Visits the Grand Canyon" can be found online under Fan Fest and was written by Rachel Bryant.

Chapter 9

65. The 1987 murder of Sarah Saganitso and subsequent trial of George Abney is so little known that I've relied on very few sources for the chapter. The *Daily Sun* did an excellent job of following both the investigation and the trial. I was also fortunate to find a person who attended several days of courtroom proceedings, and she gave me her insights. I've spoken to retired law enforcement and heard

the "opinions" of various locals, and their takes informed some of my writing. Recently I've heard two podcasts on the "Skinwalker" trial, both pretty good. However, it seems they took their information from news reports as well. If any of the story comes from outside the above sources, I will append an endnote.

66. Background information on Sarah and her murder came mainly from issues of the *Daily Sun*, June 14 through June 20, 1987. As in most newspaper articles of the time, information was repeated each issue and rehashed again when the trial began.

67. Once again, issues of the *Daily Sun* throughout much of September and October 1987 rehashed the details of Abney's life in Flagstaff, his calls to Pastor Patterson, his dreams, the confession, etc.

68. *Arizona Daily Sun*, June 16, 1988.

69. The trial of George Abney was covered by the *Arizona Daily Sun* from jury selection on June 6, 1988, to his acquittal July 19, 1988 (which was actually written up in the following day's paper, July 20). There were, of course, days when court was adjourned. The reader interested in the trial can use a newspaper.com search and find the coverage. In my opinion, the most interesting testimony was covered in the following issues of the *Sun*: June 16, 1988; June 22, 1988; June 26, 1988; July 3, 1988; and July 20, 1988.

BIBLIOGRAPHY

Newspapers

Apache County Critic
Arizona Champion
Arizona Daily Sun
Coconino Sun
Coconino Weekly Sun
The Lumberjack
St. John's Herald
Tucson Citizen

Pamphlets and Papers

National Transportation Safety Board. "Midair Collision, Accident Investigation Report…June 30, 1956." File Name: 1956-06-30-US.pdf. www.fss.aero.
Northern Arizona Pioneers' Historical Society. "Calvary Catholic Cemetery Tour: Who Lies Beneath?" October 8, 2017.
———. "Headstone History—Who Lies Beneath?" October 14, 2018.
———. "Sinners, Saints, and Settlers—A Tour of Flagstaff's South Side." September 19, 2015.
Shock, Donald Paul. "The History of Flagstaff." Thesis, University of Arizona, 1952.

Bibliography

Books and Articles

Brady, Margaret. *"Some Kind of Power": Navajo Children's Skinwalker Narratives*. Salt Lake City: University of Utah Press, 1984.

Bruner, Betsy. "Up Close: Lively Rebuilding Son's Memory." *Arizona Daily Sun*, February 22, 2010.

Cline, Platt. *Mountain Town, Flagstaff's First Century*. Flagstaff, AZ: Northland Publishing, 1994.

———. *They Came to the Mountain*. Flagstaff: Northern Arizona University with Northland Publishing, 1976.

"Collision and Air Safety: The Lessons of Grand Canyon." *LIFE*, April 29, 1957.

Hudson, John C. "Towns of the Western Railroads." *Great Plains Quarterly* 2, no. 1 (Winter 1982): 41–54.

Johnson, Susan. *Flagstaff's Walkup Family Murders: A Shocking 1937 Tragedy*. Charleston, SC: The History Press, 2021.

Lankford, Andrea. *Haunted Hikes*. Solana Beach, CA: Santa Monica Press, 2006.

Magnum, Richard, and Sherry Magnum. *Flagstaff Past & Present*. Flagstaff, AZ: Northland Publishing, 2003.

Nelson, Mike. *We Are Going In: The Story of the 1956 Grand Canyon Collison*. Tucson, AZ: Rio Nuevo Publishers, 2012.

Wittig, Stacey. "Exploring Flagstaff's Forgotten Underground." *Flagstaff Business News*, February 16, 2016. www.flagstaffbusinessnews.com.

Podcasts

Bauer, Michael. "TWA Flight 2/United Flight 718 (1956 Grand Canyon.)" *Plane Crash Podcast*. Podcast audio. March 25, 2021. Apple App.

King, C.R. "Commodore Perry Owens, Lawmen." *True Stories of the Old West*. Podcast audio. April 18, 2022. Apple App.

Sparkman, Michael. "Commodore Perry Owens & The Pleasant Valley War." *Wild West Extravaganza*. Podcast audio. June 14, 2021. Apple App.

Warner, Robyn. "Episode 249—Sarah Saganitso." *The Trail Went Cold*. Podcast audio. October 26, 2021. Apple App.

BIBLIOGRAPHY

Websites, Etc.

Admiral Cloudberg. "Into the Abyss: The 1956 Grand Canyon Mid-air Collision." *Medium*, October 23, 2021. https://admiralcloudberg.medium.com.

Alexander, Kathy. "Commodore Perry Owens, Gunfighting Lawman." Legends of America, www.legendsofamerica.com.

Bryant, Rachel. "A Journey into the Haunted Visits the 'Grand Canyon.'" fanfest.com.

Charnstrom, Nikki. "The Forgotten Underground." Documentary film, January 2016.

Coveney, Katlyn. "Flagstaff Tunnels Lead to a Mysterious Past." *Lumberjack*, April 28, 2017. jackcentral.org.

Library of Congress. "Chronicling America—Historic American Newspapers." *Coconino Sun*. https://chroniclingamerica.loc.gov.

Library of Congress, Sanborn Fire Insurance Maps.

Navajo County Historical Museum. Holbrook, Arizona.

Newspapers.com.

Ramsdell, Claire. "Folklore, Legends, and Mysteries of Flagstaff, Arizona." Detour Effect. June 2021. https://thedetoureffect.com.

Surette, Justin. "The Story of the 1956 Grand Canyon Mid-Air Collision." Simple Flying, March 24, 2023. https://simpleflying.com.

Trimble, Marshall. "In His Own Words: Sheriff Commodore Perry Owens." *True West*, August 10, 2021. https://truewestmagazine.com.

Weatherford Hotel. weatherfordhotel.com.

Wikipedia. "Air Crash over the Grand Canyon." en.m.wikipedia.org.

———. "Arizona Territorial Legislature—Sessions." en.m.wikipedia.org.

———. "Commodore Perry Owens." en.m.wikipedia.org.

YouTube. "The Forgotten Underground Film." Nikki Charnstrom, 2016.

ABOUT THE AUTHOR

This is Susan Johnson's third book about her adopted hometown of Flagstaff for The History Press. While she has lived a conventional life, Susan enjoys rummaging through the hidden secrets and dusty corners of the town's past. She especially likes uncovering the quirky, haunted and wicked tales that Flagstaff—like all towns—has tucked away in its archives.

When not sitting at her computer, Susan can be found out on the trails with her faithful corgi Shimmer. She also helps her son Nick with Freaky Foot Tours and enjoys walking historic downtown in the moonlight.

Visit us at
www.historypress.com